# Fashion with Leather

# Fashion with Leather

Kate Leather

B T Batsford Ltd  London

To John, Stephen and William

# Acknowledgment

I should like to express my thanks to Sue Spiller for transforming my
hurried hieroglyphics into attractive illustrations, to Peter Alexander
Lloyd for the photography, and to Joan Green, Betty Butler and
Jane Hill for typing the manuscript.

KL Derby 1977

Set in Century IBM by Tek-Art (Typesetting) Ltd

Printed in Great Britain by
The Anchor Press Limited, Tiptree, Essex
for the publishers
B T Batsford Ltd
4 Fitzhardinge Street
London W1H 0AH

# Contents

# Preface

Leather and suede are luxurious and desirable materials, and even though they are expensive, they are not difficult to work.

This book is intended mainly for fashion-conscious readers who have some basic knowledge of sewing and dressmaking and who would like to bring to their clothes the impact and originality which suede and leather can give.

I have tried not to be too technical, and have used equipment and materials which are easily available, and methods which most people who dressmake will understand.

The majority of the ideas suggested have been made from smallish skins, or off-cuts of suede and leather, and all have been made on a domestic swing-needle sewing machine.

Although patterns are given for various items illustrated, try to use these only as basic shapes for your own ideas. When you begin to handle and use the suede and leather, I am sure that many variations will suggest themselves and enable you to bring to your work originality and creativity which will make it truly individual.

Kate Leather
Derby 1977

# Introduction

The use of suede and leather in fashion has acquired a new importance in the last few years. Young designers have used this material in ways which appear to be new but, looking back through history, we find it has been used for clothing since the emergence of man as a hunter.

As time passed, man found ways of preserving animal skin, thus he was able to develop its use, which in many ways changed his life style. By hardening the skin, he produced bowls and containers of many kinds. His first boat was a coracle made from a wooden frame with skin stretched over it. When men made their first permanent homes, skins covered roofs and doorways rendering them waterproof; the same material lined the walls inside, making them warmer and decorative. Man made leather bags in which to carry water. This enabled him to move away from the streams and springs on which he depended, thus widening his hunting area.

As the centuries progressed more and more articles were made from leather: coaches, sedan chairs, lamps, lanterns, furniture and musical instruments. During the Tudor period, leather clothing became fashionable for people of wealth. Until this time it had been used only by workmen who needed clothes to give protection or for heavy wear. Now it was embroidered and decorated to produce opulent jackets, waistcoats, gloves and shoes.

During the Industrial Revolution leather was introduced as driving belts for the new machinery, and great quantities were used for upholstery in railway carriages.

We are all familiar with the extensive use of leather in the Wild West period: leather saddles, holsters and all types of clothing. Indirectly this caused the buffalo to disappear from the American plains, the resident Indians lost their main source of food, and so began the Indian uprising against the settlers.

The leather trade has given new words to the English language. Marines are called 'leather necks' because in early times their neck stocks were made from leather. A naughty child received a 'tanning' because the belt or strap used to administer punishment was processed by the tanning method. The pale yellow colour called 'buff' is so called because it was the colour produced when the hide of the European buffalo was dressed by the shamoying method.

When it is realized how important leather has been to man's development throughout the centuries, it is hardly surprising that dress designers constantly return to this material. Modern suedes and leathers are now made in many weights and colours, and continued research has enabled manufacturers to produce printed and embossed skins which have been used with great effect by current designers.

It is not difficult to work with suede and leather. Little specialised equipment is needed and with the knowledge of a few basic techniques these materials can be introduced into clothes and accessories most successfully.

# 1 Techniques

## BEFORE BUYING A SKIN

Leather and suede can be bought in many weights and finishes, and are usually graded for quality. Grading refers to the usable quantity of the skin and not the quality of tanning. A grade 'A' skin therefore has the highest proportion of perfect surface area. However, knowledge of the skin formation of leather will help to make the maximum use of any skin.

Size

A large proportion of leather used is sheep skin. These skins are roughly 0.46 m² - 0.65 m² (5 - 7 sq ft). Calf and cow skins are 1.86 m² - 5.57 m² (20 - 60 sq ft) in area, and are sold in several ways:

(a)   the entire skin
(b)   a side — half skin cut along the back bone
(c)   the belly — the irregular under part of the skin
(d)   the back — the area either side of the back bone.

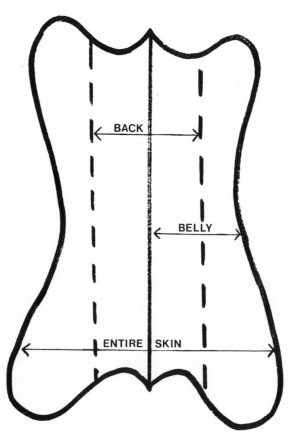

1    *Shape of complete skin showing parts*

## Strength

In all skins, the finest grain, and therefore the strongest part of the skin, lies along, and either side of, the back bone. The underside of the skin has the largest grain and is often irregular and less stable in texture. It is coarser and stretches more in wear.

The strength of the skin is important. Soft leathers are subject to tearing, and weak areas in heavier skins should be avoided for positions of heavy wear in garments. Skins should, therefore, be examined carefully before use.

## Nap

The surface finish of suede and leather may have a nap. If the leather is finished on the grain or 'shiny' side, it has no 'nap', but if it has a scaled surface, eg alligator, crocodile, snake skin, or other textured surface, the leather may have to be cut 'one way'.

Similarly suede surfaces may have a 'napped' finish, and may 'shade' in the finished article if not cut correctly. The way of determining 'nap' on suede is the same as that for any fabric. Simply pass the hand over the pile in one direction, and then back again in the opposite direction. Note any difference in colour, and whether there is a rougher feeling in one direction or the other. If so, the suede has a 'nap' which will have to be noted when placing pattern pieces.

## Quantity

It is often difficult to estimate the amount of skin needed. If it is being bought locally, the pattern could be taken along to the shop when the skin is being purchased, especially if the article or garment being made is fairly small. A copy of the pattern could also be sent if buying by mail order. Most suppliers are understanding and help as much as they can.

However, it is possible to convert fabric amounts into skin quantity by multiplying the number of square metres/feet of the fabric width, by the number of metres/yards, and adding a little extra for irregularities in the skins. In most places leather is measured and sold in square feet.

1 yd (90 cm) x 54 in. (140 cm) = 13 sq ft (1.21 m$^2$).

If the garment needs 2 yd (180 cm) of 54 in. (140 cm) fabric, multiply 2 yd (180 cm) by 13 (1.21) which equals 26 sq ft (2.42 m$^2$). Add 2 sq ft (0.19 m$^2$) for every yard (90 cm) of fabric, (this is for piecing due to flaws in the skin).

26 sq ft (2.42 m$^2$) plus 4 sq ft (0.37 m$^2$) equals 30 sq ft (2.79 m$^2$)

Therefore a garment needing 2 yd of 54 in. fabric would need the equivalent of 30 sq ft (2.79 m$^2$) of suede or leather.

## CHOOSING A DESIGN

The choice of design for suede and leather needs some forethought. Leathers can be soft and supple, lending themselves to tucked and gathered designs, or rugged and sturdy, needing a sharper style to bring out the quality of the skin.

When choosing a design, think of the weight and appearance of the skin, and how well it will adapt to the chosen style. Will it fall softly into gathers for evening wear? Has it enough body to retain the square cut look of a short flared jacket? The same standards

2    *Evening dress with bodice and shoulder strap straps in soft suede*

3    *Short jacket in medium to heavyweight skin, with top-stitching*

apply as when choosing fabric for any garment: match the weight and characteristics of the fabric to the style and lines of the design (figures 2 and 3).

*4   Styles suitable for skin, showing seaming as part of the design*

If the skin is being used with other fabric, as a yoke or pocket flap, for example, try to match the weight and feeling of the skin to that of the main fabric. This will produce a more professional result, and help to eliminate technical problems in the construction of the garment.

### Size

As limitations are imposed by the size of the skins, designs that 'cut-up' the figure — ie with shoulder yokes, panelled bodices, waist seams, gored skirts, hip yokes, — are more economical for leather and suede than styles which have large pattern pieces. Many of these features can be introduced into patterns, especially if the skin is to be used with other fabric. However, care should be taken that the finished garment does not look 'patchy', with the skin placed haphazardly, in relation to the balance of the whole design. (figure 4).

5    *Raglan and kimono
sleeved jacket*

### Easing

Leather and suede do not 'ease' particularly well, so for all but the
very soft, supple skins, designs featuring raglan or kimono sleeves
are often more successful (figure 5).

If a set-in sleeve is used, reduction of the 'ease' in the sleeve head
often gives better results (figure 6).

When 'easing' is accomplished in the form of a dart, this can be
done in one of two ways. *Either* the area of suppression can be
extended — eg 2.5 cm (1 in.) elbow dart can be extended over 5 cm
(2 in.) *or* the dart can be included in a seam. This is particularly
effective in bodice sections (figure 7).

### Topstitching

Designs which feature top-stitching are often perfect for suede and
leather. Not only is it a very suitable and classic form of trimming,
but top-stitching provides a means of flattening seams. This is doubly
important as the normal pressing procedure is not possible with skin
(figure 8).

6    *Reduction of 'ease' in a set-in sleeve*

7    *Sleeve dart extended in the form of easing over a larger area*

8    *Areas where top-stitching can be used to great advantage*

## PROBLEMS TURNED TO ADVANTAGE

When designing, or choosing a pattern for a garment or article to be made in skin, the techniques of producing that design should be understood.

Facings made from skin often present problems in coats and jackets. They can be heavy both in weight and appearance. The repeated handling of skin in this area breaks up the fibres and produces a dusty surface called 'crocking' and it may be more comfortable in wear not to have skin facings.

To introduce other fabrics for facings will not only reduce these, and several other problems, but could also add to the impact of the design.

Jersey, silk, tweed or other suitable fabrics could be used for revers facings and collars.

Embroidered ribbons provide decorative facings to openings and edges on both adults' and children's clothing.

Grosgrain ribbon on the inside of cuffs and waistbands.

Soft fabric to face necklines and armholes.

Lining to turn up hems.

All these add to comfort in wear, and a more professional look to the finished garment.

Many commercial patterns are designed to be made entirely in skin, or have suede and leather listed in the suggested fabrics. These patterns are, of course, very good, and this makes the choice of a design fairly simple. However, it is possible to adapt and adjust other styles and ideas to the characteristics of skin, and, with a little practice, to introduce personal variations, and so experience the excitement and satisfaction of creating something individual.

## SIMPLE EQUIPMENT

It is not necessary to have great quantities of specialized equipment. Just add to existing equipment whatever will make the sewing of suede and leather easier. (figure 9).

*Sharp scissors* with shortish blades will cut all skins, except the very heavy ones.

*Skiving knife* or a safety razor blade is used for thinning the edges of leather and reducing bulk.

*Hole punchers* and eyelet tools are useful for fastenings and decorative features.

*A wooden mallet*, or a hammer covered with padding, for flattening seams and edges.

*Leather needles* for machine, and glovers needles for hand-stitching, make the sewing of skins easier. Normal machine needles, size 14-16 (90-100) — depending on the weight of the leather — are also suitable.

*Thread* needs to be strong, and of a suitable weight for the skin. Pure

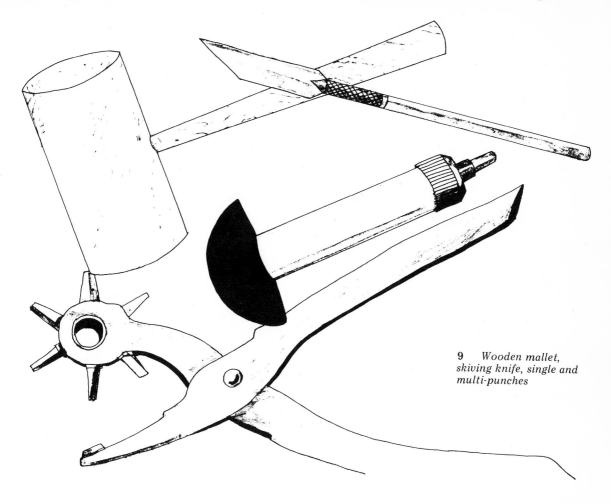

9    *Wooden mallet,
skiving knife, single and
multi-punches*

silk is good for normal sewing, also mercerized and polyester threads. Top-stitching is most effective in silk buttonhole twist. Thread coated with beeswax prevents tangling when hand sewing.

*Masking tape* or single and double-sided Sellotape, for holding seams, pockets, etc, in position temporarily, and as a substitute for tacking.

*Sewing machines* need to be tested before use. Foot pressure may need to be reduced if the skin is thick. Thread tension should also be checked. Length of stitch is important, as a stitch which is too small may cause tearing at the seams. 7-10 stitches per 2.5 cm (1 in.) is usually successful. A smooth-running, clean machine is a great asset, so it is worth spending time in preparation.

## CONSTRUCTION

*Toile* Because of the special characteristics of leather and suede, and the expense involved, it is sensible to try out the fit and shape of any garment before cutting into the skins. This trial run is called a toile, and is done in all fashion houses irrespective of the final fabric.

Choose a toile fabric which will behave in much the same way as the skin. A heavy cotton, or firmly woven muslin are good if the skin is light to medium weight. Non-woven interfacing, and cotton felt are preferable if a heavier skin is to be used.

The making of a toile may seem unnecessary extra work, but the fit, shape and balance of the garment can be checked, and altered as required; design adjustments, or decorative addition, can be tested; the type of seam treatment, and other processes can be decided and tried out — all before the skin is touched.

This means that the making of the actual garment will be much quicker and the final result more professional, since the skin will not have been over-handled.

Remember, every stitch shows in leather, unpicked seams will leave marks which cannot be removed.

### Preparing the skin

Get to know the feel and quality of the skin.

Handle it, pull in all directions to see where it stretches, where the flaws are, and then use the skin to its maximum advantage.

Mark any holes, scars, or colour irregularities on the wrong side, so that they can be avoided when placing the pattern. Sometimes, however, these flaws can be used to advantage and often enhance the casual ruggedness of, for instance, a sports garment.

Areas of the skin that stretch should be used in the garment where stretch is most needed, eg side bodice panels, sleeve heads, shoulder yokes, etc.

### Pattern layout

After the skin has been examined and marked in this way the pattern can be placed in position. (figure 10).

Alterations at the toile stage should be transfered onto the pattern; alternatively the toile can be taken apart and used as the pattern.

Determine if the skin has a nap by the method already suggested. If it has, take care to place the pattern pieces with the nap running in the same direction on each one. Marking the top of each pattern piece will help you to remember this.

The strongest and most evenly textured area of the skin lies alongside the backbone of the animal. Place the most important pattern pieces in this area, eg bodice, skirt, sleeve. The side parts of the skin can be used for smaller pattern pieces and facings.

Try to use the skin to maximum advantage; place the strongest

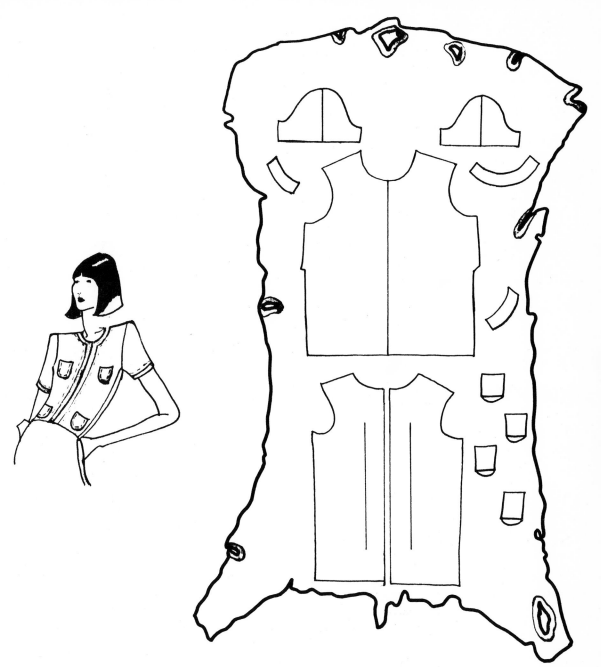

10    *Skin with faulty areas
marked and pattern pieces
in position*

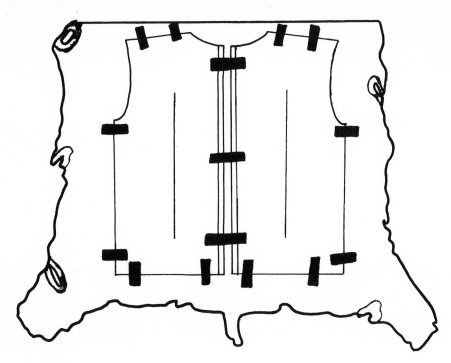

11   *Pattern pieces held with masking tape*

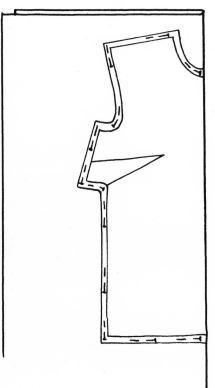

12   *Pattern piece placed to a fold on very soft skin. Note that pins are placed in the seam allowance*

parts of the skin where they will receive most wear in the garment. Use the outer area for less important pieces, or where the stretch in this part of the skin will be of use, eg for side bodices, easing etc.

Skin will form permanent creases in wear at elbow and knee, making sleeves and trousers shorter. Extra length, approximately 2.5 cm (1 in.) added to these pieces will prevent this happening.

Apart from nap consideration, pattern pieces can be placed in any direction. This is especially so on smooth leathers, and when working with small pattern pieces. The pattern should be placed on the wrong side of the skin.

When the layout has been planned satisfactorily some method must be found to keep the pattern in position to ensure accurate cutting. On smooth leathers and fine suedes pins will leave marks, so I would suggest:

(a)  Placing small pieces of Sellotape over the edges of the pattern at regular intervals on the wrong side of the skin.

(b)  Outlining the pattern with soft pencil or felt tipped pen on the wrong side of the skin, removing the pattern before cutting. When using this method, the pattern pieces are cut singly. Reverse sleeves, bodices, etc, so that sections are cut in pairs, and not two of a kind. Where a section should be placed to a fold, trace round the pattern and fold line, then turn the pattern over, lay it along the fold line again, and trace the opposite side.

(c)  Dressmaker's weights.

When using very soft skins, particularly suede, the skin can be lightly folded, so as not to make a crease, and the pattern pinned with silk pins in the seam allowance. Any marks that are made here by the pins will not be visible in the finished garment.

## Cutting

Sharp dressmaking shears will cut most skins. Use a smooth, even action to avoid jagged edges. Wherever possible, avoid picking up the skin to cut it.

## Marking-up

Most marking, eg darts, seam allowances, pocket positions, etc, can be done on the wrong side with a soft pencil or felt-tipped pen and a ruler. Test that the marking will not show through onto the right side of the skin. Tailor's tacks will leave marks on the right side of leathers.

## Tacking

The garment should not need to be tacked in the normal way if a toile has been made and fitted, and alterations and adjustments made.

However, seams and design features will need to be held in position temporarily, for accurate machining.

Paper clips, or staples placed in the seam allowances, will hold straight seams (figure 13).

Transparent or masking tape can also be used. Check the effect of tape on the skin. It may mark a suede surface, or pull off surface grain on leather. If it is suitable for use on the skin, machining can continue through the tape and the remainder pulled off afterwards (figure 14).

Over-layed seams can be held in position by rubber cement. Apply cement to appropriate seam allowances, allow to dry, then place glued areas together in final position. Layers can be taken apart and repositioned before machining, if necessary. (figure 15).

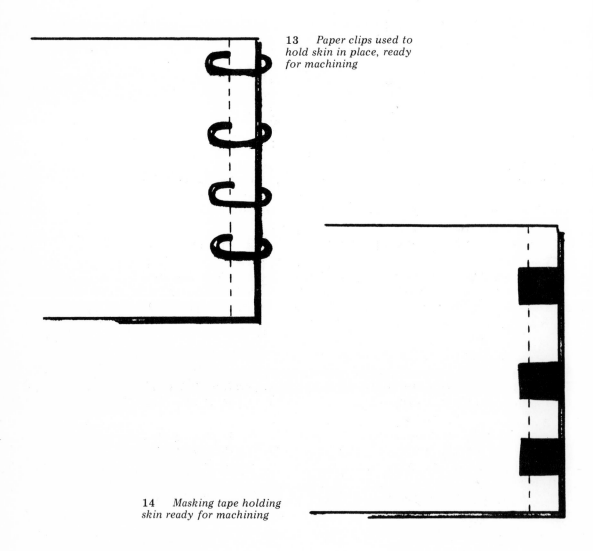

13  *Paper clips used to hold skin in place, ready for machining*

14  *Masking tape holding skin ready for machining*

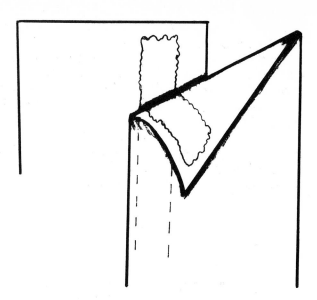

**15**    *Rubber cement used for overlayed seams*

## Machining

If the machine has been checked for correct needle, thread, and length of stitch, machining skin is no more difficult than other fabrics. Straight seams are best machined in a top to bottom direction. Tie off the ends as back stitching often tears the skin. Do not machine too quickly; a uniform speed will assure even stitches. Machines which have a slow gear make this easier. Shiny skins may need tissue paper between them and the pressure foot for top-stitching. Masking tape could also be used, providing it does not damage the surface of the skin. Some machines have a roller or a silicon-coated foot, which can also be used.

## Seams

Most traditional seams can be used on skin, together with several adaptations which are particularly suitable. The weight of skin and type of garment will determine choice of seam.

Over-lapping, top-stitched seams are best when using heavy skins. This type of leather is soft and bulky and will not fold or flatten easily. Soft, lightweight skins need traditional treatment for support and finish.

Test the type of seam chosen before making a final decision. Adjust seam allowance to the type of skin.

*Plain seam*
Baste skin together by one of the specialist methods previously des-
cribed, right side to right side.
    Stitch on fitting line.
    Open seam allowance on wrong side.
    Flatten by hammering, and glue seam allowance in position if
necessary (figure 16).

*Taped seam*
This is a plain seam, taped for extra strength and reinforcement.
    Baste seam right side to right side.
    Place pre-shrunk tape along fitted line.
    Stitch through tape and skin.
    Flatten as for plain seam (figure 17).

*Top-stitched seam*
A versatile seam, as it flattens and decorates in addition to constructing.

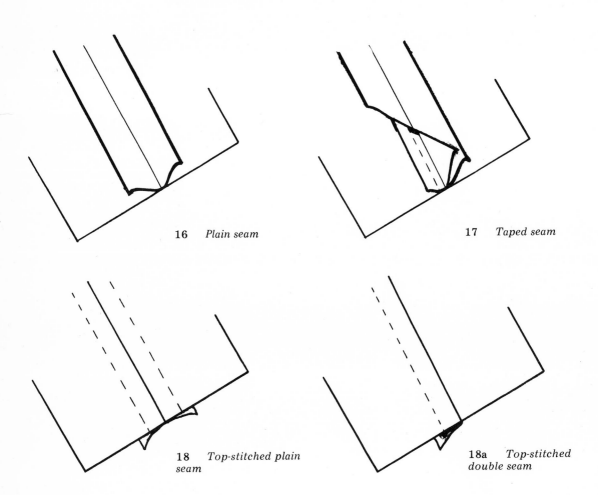

16    *Plain seam*

17    *Taped seam*

18    *Top-stitched plain
seam*

18a    *Top-stitched
double seam*

Baste seam right side to right side. Stitch along fitting line.

Two methods of top-stitching can then be used:

(a)    open seam allowance as for plain seam, and top-stitch either side of seam line, working from the right side.

(b)    hammer both seam allowances to one side of seam line. Stitch through top of garment and both seam allowances, working from the right side, producing one line of top-stitching on the seam.

The width of the top-stitched line in both methods will depend on the style of garment and weight of skin (figures 18 and 18a).

*Overlayed seam*

This seam is particularly easy to work and most suitable for medium and heavy weight, as it reduces bulk (figure 19).

Trim away seam allowance back to the fitting line on one side of the garment. This is usually on the front so that the seam lies towards the back of the garment in wear, but the choice is optional.

Place cut edge along the fitting line of the remaining section,

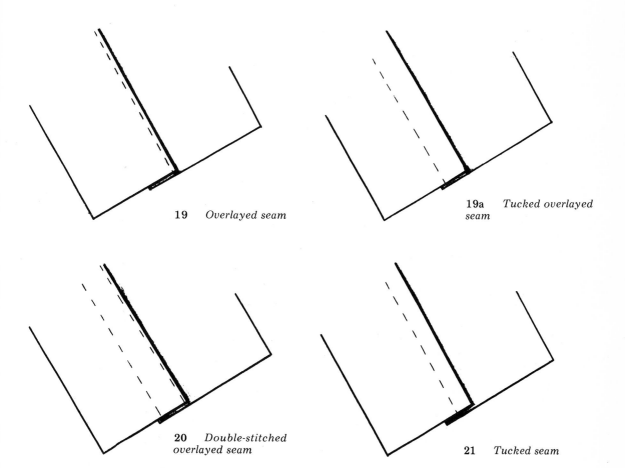

19    *Overlayed seam*

19a    *Tucked overlayed seam*

20    *Double-stitched overlayed seam*

21    *Tucked seam*

working from the right side. Glue lightly in position.

Top-stitch close to the cut edge, working through both layers.

The line of top-stitching can be made 1-2 cm (¼-½ in.) from the cut edge, to produce a tucked seam effect (figure 19a).

Two lines of top-stitching, one close to the trimmed edge, and approximately 1 cm (½ in.) in, produces a decorative effect, most suitable when the seams of the design need to be emphasized (figure 20).

### Welt seam

This has the appearance of a top-stitched seam, but is less bulky.

Baste, and stitch along fitted line.

Hammer both seam allowances to one side of seam line.

Trim away top seam allowance close to fitting line.

Top stitch from the right side, working through garment and lower seam allowance, encasing trimmed seam allowance.

### Tucked seam

Another seam which is decorative, as well as constructional, and one which is particularly effective in light weight skin.

Fold back seam allowance to the fitting line on one side of the garment, working from the right side. The fold can be hammered to flatten if desired.

Place folded edge along fitting line of remaining section of garment, and stitch 1 cm (½ in.) in from the folded edge.

This seam is very attractive when used with yokes and inset sections (figure 21).

### Flat-felled seam

This is a useful seam to use if the garment is to be unlined as it is completely self neatening.

Baste seam wrong side to wrong side and stitch a plain seam.

Turn seam allowances to one side and hammer flat.

Trim close to stitching line on lower seam allowance.

Turn in edge of upper seam allowance and place over trimmed seam allowance, completely enclosing it. Hammer flat.

Top stitch onto garment through all thicknesses (figure 22).

### Chanel seam

A slightly more complicated seam, but one which provides an opportunity for many variations. This seam can be produced in two ways, depending on the effect required, and the weight of the skin being used.

### Method 1    Overlayed chanel seam

Trim away seam allowance to the fitting line on both sections to be joined.

Cut a backing strip approximately 2.5 cm (1 in.) wide and as long

2222222

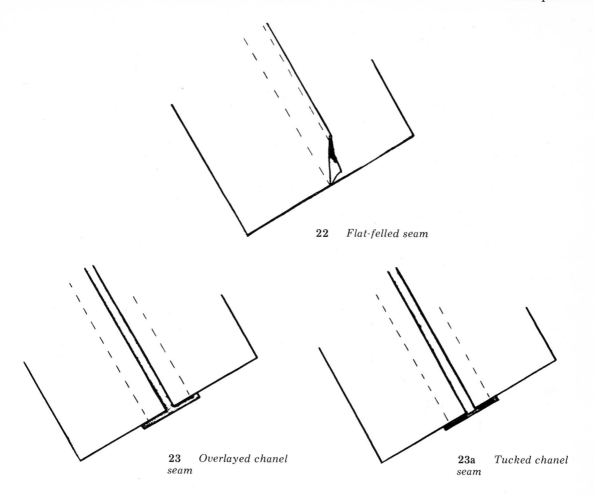

22  *Flat-felled seam*

23  *Overlayed chanel seam*

23a  *Tucked chanel seam*

as required.

Place the two trimmed edges together so that they lie down the centre of the backing strip.

Stitch 1 cm (½ in.) in from the cut edges (figure 23).

*Method 2  Tucked chanel seam*

Fold back seam allowance to the fitting line on both sections to be joined.

Cut back strip approximately 2.5 cm (1 in.) wide and as long as required.

Place the two folded edges together so that they lie down the centre of the backing strip.

Stitch 1 cm (½ in.) in from the folded edge.

The folded edges produce a more emphasized effect than the cut edges in this seam (figure 23a).

The backing strip can be cut from contrasting skins or fabric, or in a contrasting colour, to produce an even greater decorative effect.

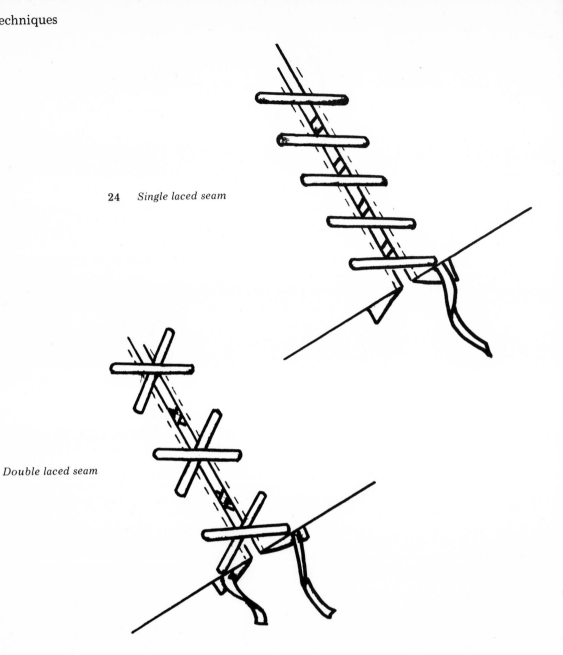

24    *Single laced seam*

24a    *Double laced seam*

*Laced seam*
This finish is particularly suitable for use with suede and leather as it produces the rustic effect so often associated with skin, but it can also be used successfully with more sophisticated styles (figures 24 and 24a).
Mark the position of the holes on both the sections to be joined.

Generally the holes are evenly spaced, but the position will depend on the lacing design. If the skin is lightweight, or has a degree of stretch, the area carrying the holes will have to be reinforced with interfacing on the wrong side.

Punch holes. Purchased metal eyelets could be used at this stage to reinforce the lacing holes.

Lace the two sections together with narrow leather strips, ribbons, cord, shoe laces, etc. Tie off ends firmly.

Overlayed seams, tucked seams, chanel seams can all be variations of a laced seam, by lacing instead of stitching.

*Pressing and flattening seams*
Pressing in the normal way is not possible with skin, so other methods of flattening seams must be used. Rubber cement can be used effectively.

Pound the fold or seam allowance with mallet, or fabric covered hammer, to 'set' crease.

Apply cement to both surfaces, and allow to dry before sticking together (figure 25).

Hammer again on the glued area so that both surfaces stick together.

Gently lift outer edge of seam allowance to prevent ridge on right side.

Choose a cement which manufacturers state will be suitable for skin, and follow directions carefully. Do not be over generous with glue as this may seep through onto the right side and stain the surface.

Never stitch over cement which is exposed on the surface, or has not dried.

If the garment has a dart which is not included in a seam, stitch in the usual way, being extra careful to taper out the stitching.

Trim dart to approximately 1 cm (½ in.) from stitching.

Hammer over a curved pressing ham, and glue in position (figure 26).

Skiving also has the effect of flattening seams (figure 27). This process in leather is the same as that of grading seams in other fabric. It reduces bulk on seams, and should be used wherever this is necessary in a garment. This process can be done using a special knife, or with a safety razor blade.

Cut from the wrong side making a diagonal cut. Long continuous strips can be joined with a skived edge and either stuck or machined together.

Reduce bulk wherever possible; this should be done even when skiving is not a suitable method. Curved edges and seams should be notched, and corners mitred, to produce good shapes (figures 28 and 29).

A warm, dry iron can sometimes be used on leather, providing always that the skin is protected with a dry pressing cloth or brown paper. It is also possible to use this method on some suedes, but always test a small piece, whatever the type of skin.

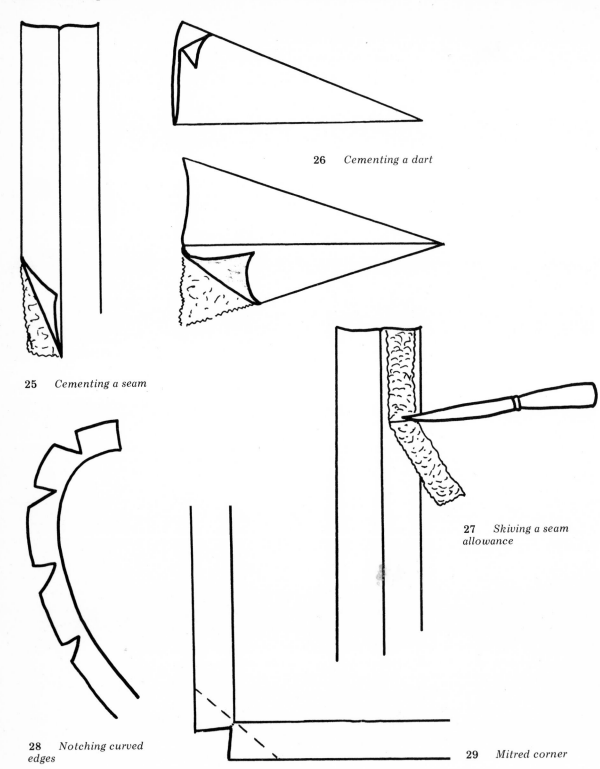

25    *Cementing a seam*

26    *Cementing a dart*

27    *Skiving a seam allowance*

28    *Notching curved edges*

29    *Mitred corner*

## Interfacing

Although most skins are firm, they may still need the support of interfacing in certain areas to retain their shape and strength. Necklines, buttonholes, cuffs, openings and hemlines are all improved by the use of interfacings. Lightweight, non-woven interfacings give good results and are easy to work with. Always match weight of interfacing to weight of skin. Lightweight, fusible interfacings can be used if applied with dry heat. Use them to stabilize edges and shapes (eg front-edged waistcoat and shapes for appliqué) and to reinforce thin areas of skin.

## Openings and fastenings

Many traditional methods of fastenings can be used on skin, but there is also tremendous scope for adapting these methods, and producing something new and particularly suitable for leather and suede.

Openings and fastenings should be simple, and bulk should be reduced wherever possible.

Buttons and buttonholes make a suitable type of fastening, and so do zips, studs, lacings, frogs and toggles.

Haberdashery counters are a continual source of new ideas.

### Buttonholes

To make a buttonhole in leather or suede may seem a little daunting, but with practice, and the adaptation of more traditional methods, it is no more difficult than in any other material.

*Handworked buttonholes*  These are worked in the same way as for any other fabric.

Mark the size and position of the buttonhole on the garment. Use a soft pencil and ruler for accurage spacing. Slash through all layers, and work with buttonhole twist.

*Machine-worked buttonholes*  These can be made on skin in the usual way. Work a test buttonhole first to check the thickness of suede or leather on the machine.

*Stitched buttonholes 1*  Because the skin does not fray, adaptations of traditional methods can be used.

When the garment is completed, and the facing is in place, mark the size and position of the buttonhole on the facing with a soft pencil.

Machine along the rectangle and tie off the thread on the wrong side.

Slash between the lines of machining (figures 30 and 30a).

*Stitched buttonholes 2*  Cut a rectangle the size of the buttonhole from the right side of the garment (single layer only).

Glue round the edges of this rectangle on the wrong side.

facing

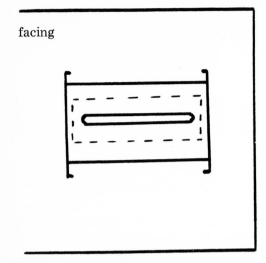

**30**   *Stitched button-hole 1 — marking posi-tion on facing*

R.S. garment

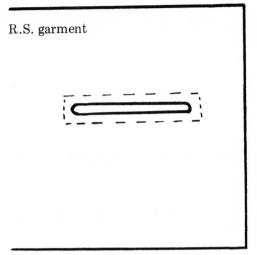

**30a**   *Stitched button-hole 1 — completed buttonhole on RS of garment*

W.S.

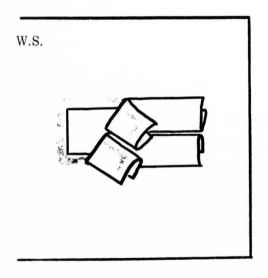

**31**   *Stitched button-hole 2 — bindings glued into position on WS of garment*

R.S.

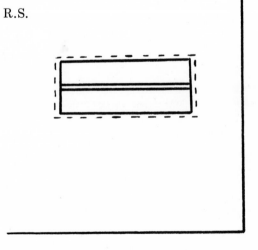

**31a**   *Stitched button-hole 2 — completed buttonhole on RS of garment*

Cut two strips of binding for each buttonhole approximately 2.5 cm (1 in.) larger than the opening, and 4 cm (1½ in. approx.) wide.

Fold each strip lengthwise, hammer, glue and flatten.

Place strips in position on the wrong side of buttonhole so that the folded edges meet lengthwise.

Glue bindings in position (figure 31).

Fold facing back, and from the right side stitch round cut rectangle.

Machine through the right side of garment, buttonhole bindings and facing of garment.

Trim away facing carefully inside stitching (figure 31a).

*Bound buttonholes* made in a traditional manner are also quite suitable for skin. A more successful result is achieved if the bindings are cut from the thinner areas of skin, or, if this is not possible or desirable, from some other fabric, eg jersey or soft wool.

*Zips*

These are a most convenient method of fastening suede and leather, and easy to handle when adaptations of standard methods are used.

*Even seam*    Fold seam allowance back onto the wrong side, hammer and glue into position.

Apply masking tape on the right side to hold folded edges together (figure 32).

Position zip on the wrong side so that the teeth lie centrally underneath the folded edges. Hold in place with tape attached to seam allowance (figure 32a).

Machine form the wrong side.

*Lapped seam*    Fold seam allowances back onto the wrong side, hammer and glue into position.

Place one folded seam edge alongside the teeth of the zip. Machine, using zip foot, from the right side.

Place second folded seam edge to cover the zip teeth, and fractionally over the first line of machining, secure in position with tape (figure 33).

Machine in place, stitching through the masking tape, from the right side (figure 33a).

Remove masking tape when zip is finally stitched in position.

*Invisible zips*    Simply follow the manufacturer's detailed instructions which are usually on the zip pack.

*Heavy weight zips*    Traditional methods of inserting zips into heavyweight skins are not always possible, but a limitation can be turned into a design feature. Heavy, coloured plastic zips and metal zips with decorative pulls can become the outstanding feature of a garment, and

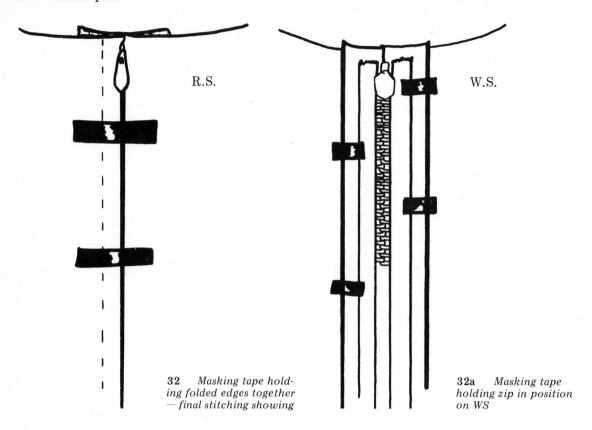

**32**   *Masking tape holding folded edges together — final stitching showing*

R.S.

**32a**   *Masking tape holding zip in position on WS*

W.S.

**33**   *Masking tape holding zip in position on WS*

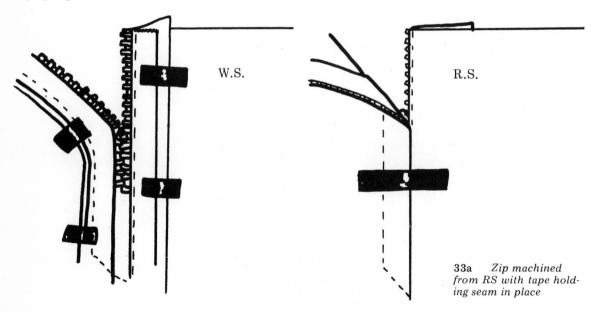

W.S.

R.S.

**33a**   *Zip machined from RS with tape holding seam in place*

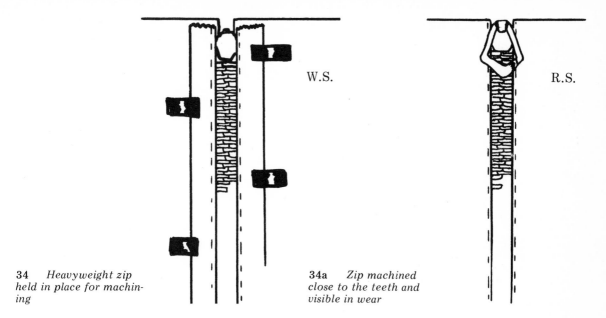

**34**  *Heavyweight zip held in place for machining*

**34a**  *Zip machined close to the teeth and visible in wear*

W.S.

R.S.

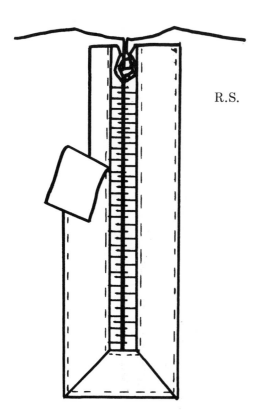

R.S.

**35**  *Zip unit with trimming tacked to zip tape*

**35a**  *Zip unit machined in position on garment, fabric behind zip teeth is trimmed away*

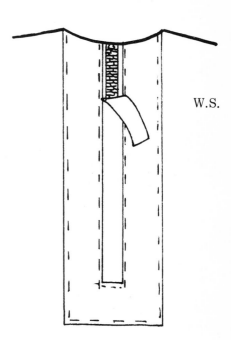

W.S.

insertion is simple if no attempt is made to conceal the zip.

Trim away the seam allowance from the opening area.

Place the newly cut edges alongside the zip teeth — hold with tape (figure 34).

Machine the garment onto the zip tape, from the right side.

Several rows of machining often increase the design feature, in addition to making the zip more secure (figure 34a).

*Inserting a zip without a seam*    This can sometimes present problems, but an easy, decorative method can be followed, using attractive ribbon or braid, or strips of contrasting leather or suede.

Tack the trimming so that it lies over the zip tape, leaving the teeth visible (figure 35).

Mitre the corners across the bottom of the zip.

Place the unit in position on the right side of the garment, where the opening is to be.

Using zip foot, machine along both edges of the trimming onto the garment.

Turn to the wrong side and cut away the rectangle of skin which lies over the zip teeth  (figure 35a).

*Lacing*

This form of fastening is very suitable for leather and suede, It has associations with the Wild West and this is part of its charm.

Variations can be introduced: loops, rings or eyelets for threading; ribbons, plaited wool and cord, leather thongs or string for ties (figures 36 and 36a).

The area that has the eyelets or holes, should be interfaced for strength (figure 36b).

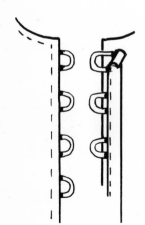

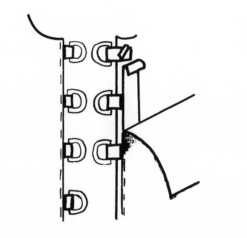

**36**    *Loops of skin or fabric for lacing*

**36a**    *Metal D rings attached by strips of skin*

**36b**    *Eyelets with re-inforcing backing strip*

*Decorative fastenings*

Buckles, straps, toggles and frogs are all suitable types of fastening and provide decoration and design features as well.

Many of these can be bought ready to use, but a little experimenting can produce variations (figure 37).

*Frogs* are made by drawing the design on paper, then pinning the cord or leather strips along the lines of the design, and sewing together where the design lines overlap (figure 38).

*Toggle loops* can be made from thin rope or cord. Make loops to go over the button, then stitch raw edges together and sew loops onto garment. Finally, cover the raw edges of cord with leather tabs (figure 39).

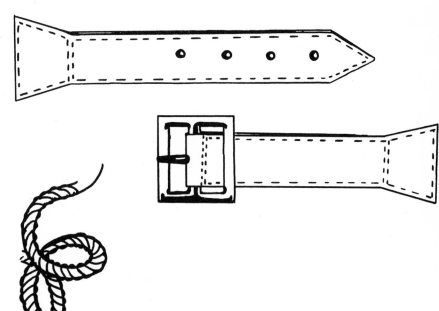

**37** *Straps made double except for the section which is stitched onto the garment*

**38** *Frogs made from cord*

**39** *Toggle loops neatened with skin shapes*

**41** *Edge to edge lining with binding*

**40** *Jacket facing taped and lining hand sewn into position*

## Linings

Although a lining may seem an added chore and expense, it really will help to keep the garment in shape. It will also make the garment much more comfortable in wear, and could add an extra touch of luxury.

Skirts and pants will probably be lined with fairly standard fabrics, but coats and jackets could be lined with quilted satin, or fur fabric, for extra warmth and style. Heavy linings could be made detachable so that the garment could be worn all the year round.

*Skirts and pants* Linings for these garments are made and stitched into position at the waistline, before the waistband is attached. The hem of the lining is left free.

*Jackets and coats* These linings are easier to manage if they are machined to the facings. If a hand-inserted lining is wanted, matching, or decorative tape should be machined to the facing, and the lining hand stitched onto this (figure 40).

*Detachable linings*    These linings can be secured to the inner edge of the facings by press studs. Short tapes, attached to the inside of the lining, with press studs on the ends which fasten onto the seam lines of the coat will help to keep the lining in position.

*Edge-to-edge linings*    This type of lining is useful when economy in the use of skin is necessary, or when it is desirable to reduce the bulk often created by skin facings. A very neat result is achieved if the edges of the garment are bound, thus securing the lining, and neatening the edge, in one process (figure 41).

Make up the garment and lining.

Place the wrong side of garment and lining together, and secure round the edges with clips.

Apply binding strips round all edges, the right side of binding to the right side of garment.

Machine through binding strip, garment and lining.

Turn binding over raw edge, and secure by further line of machining, or by hand-stitching.

## Waistbands

The waistline is an area of strain so the finish here must support the garment, be comfortable in wear and not have excessive bulk.

*Petersham*

One of the simplest ways of finishing a waist edge is to use petersham. This can be bought ready curved. Alternatively the shaping can be done by stretching what is to be the free edge, by means of a damp cloth and hot iron.

Cut the petersham approximately 8 cm (3 in.) longer than the waist measurement.

Working from the right side of the garment, pin petersham round the top of the skirt. Secure lining at this stage also (figure 42).

Extend petersham beyond waistline at each end.

Machine edge of petersham to waistline, turn in ends so that they are even with placket edges.

Neaten short ends and attach hook and eye.

Turn petersham over, to lie inside the skirt. Catch lower edge to side seam (figure 42a).

*Faced waistband*

Cut a strip of skin 8 cm (3 in.) longer than waist measurement and as wide as required.

Cut a strip of petersham ribbon 2.5 cm (1 in.) longer than the skin waistband, and slightly wider.

Place ribbon and skin with the wrong side together, turn in ribbon ends 1.5 cm (½ in.).

Machine skin waistband and ribbon together along the top length

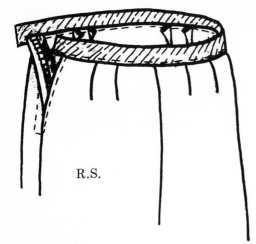

R.S.

**42**   *Petersham waist-*
*band tacked in position*
*ready for machining*

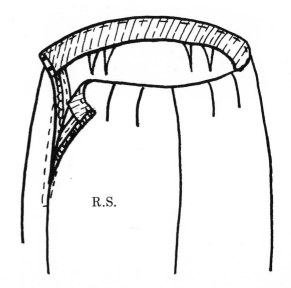

**42a**   *Petersham waist-*
*band in finished position*

R.S.

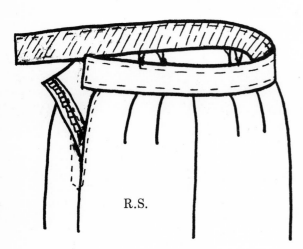

R.S.

**43**   *Waistband made*
*from skin faced with*
*petersham ribbon*

and short ends.

Place garment waistline between skin and ribbon at the lower edge of the waistband.

Position the garment so that there is an under and overwrap at the waistband.

Machine through all layers of material from the right side.

Finish with hook and eye (figure 43).

The more traditional methods of applying waistbands can also be used. Remember, always reduce bulk wherever possible. If the skin is heavy, a more satisfactory result is achieved by using fabric, eg toning wool, silk, etc, in keeping with the design.

### Hems

A little rethinking is necessary for a successful hemline in suede or leather (figure 44). The traditional pinning, tacking and hand-sewing is not possible.

Heavy skins can simply be cut to the finished length, especially if the garment is rugged and casual in design. Fringing or thonging is equally suitable for this weight of skin.

Hemlines can be faced with lining to give a neat, crisp line.

**44**    *decorative ways of finishing hemlines*

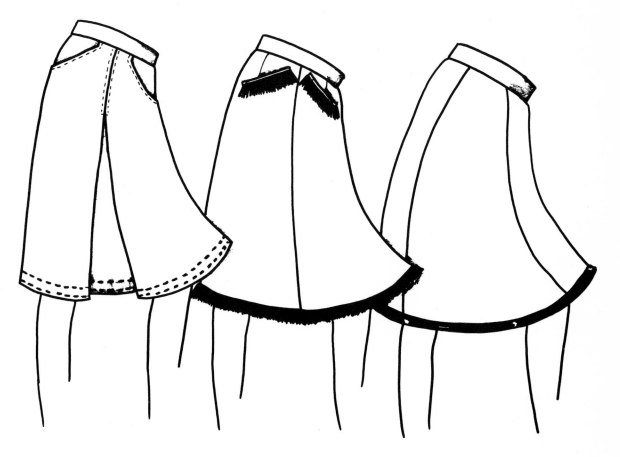

Narrow binding, made from thin leather or fabric, is another successful finish if it is in keeping with the rest of the garment.

A narrow hem 2.5 cm (1 in.) can be machined with two or three rows of stitching.

The more usual methods of turning up a hemline can also be used, with the addition of a few adaptations.

*Straight hem*
Measure the skirt length very carefully, since once the hemline crease is made, it is almost impossible to remove. Hold skirt length in position by means of clips, and hammer along crease line to set it. Remove the clips from each section as it is hammered, so that the impression is not left.

Trim hem allowance evenly. (figure 45). Straight hems may be 4 cm to 7 cm (1½ to 2½ in.) wide.

**45**    *Hemline held with paper clips and trimmed an even width*

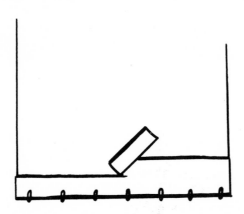

**45a**    *Adhesive appied along hem allowance*

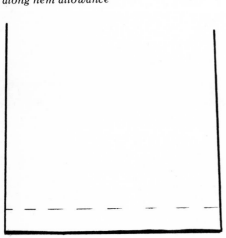

**45b**    *Hem folded into position*

Apply glue to the wrong side of hem allowance, placing it along the centre of hem allowance away from crease line and upper edge of hem allowance (figure 45a). Glue a corresponding area on the wrong side of the skirt itself.

When the glue is dry, turn up the hem allowance along the crease line, until the whole hem is in position (figure 45b). Press the glued surfaces together and hammer into final position.

*Curved hem*
Proceed as for straight hem, making hem width 2 cm to 4 cm (¾ in. to 1½ in. approx.), until hem is being folded into its final position.

To remove the fullness and make the hem allowance lie smoothly in position, snip out wedge-shaped sections to approximately 6 mm (¼ in.) above the hemline. Hammer into final position (figures 46, 46a and 46b).

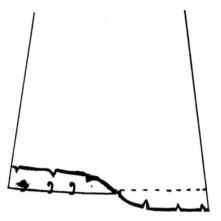

**46**   *Hemline held with paper clips and surplus skin notched away*

**46a**   *Adhesive in position*

**46b**   *Fold up hem, closing notches*

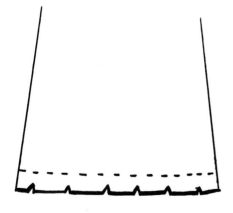

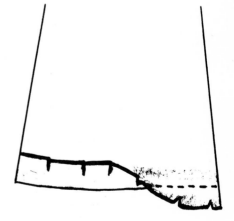

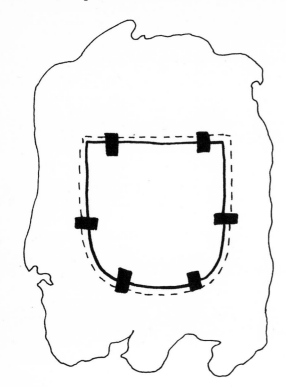

**47**  *Simple shape for unlined patch pocket*

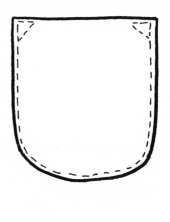

**47a**  *Method of stitching*

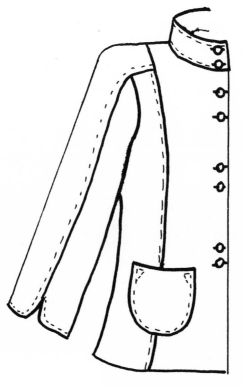

**47b**  *Positions for unlined patch posket*

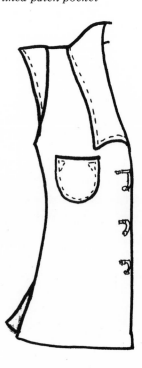

**47c**  *Positions for unlined patch pocket*

## Pockets

The simplest pockets make the most effective ones in skin. Patch, flap and welt pockets are not too difficult, especially when adaptations are made to the more usual methods of construction.

### Unlined patch pocket

Cut pocket to required size (figure 47). Do not add seam allowance. Place in position and hold temporarily with double-sided adhesive tape.

Stitch in place with one or two rows of top-stitching (figure 47a).

Reinforce top corners with a small triangle of stitching, or a decorative stud (figures 47b and 47c).

**48**   *Shape of pocket and lining*

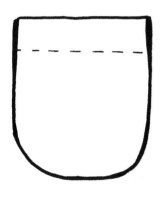

**48b**   *Pocket in position*

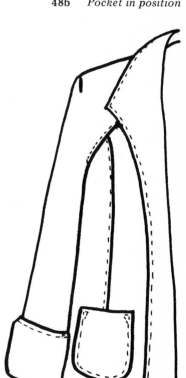

**48a**   *Pocket and lining stitched together with top slit left open for turning through*

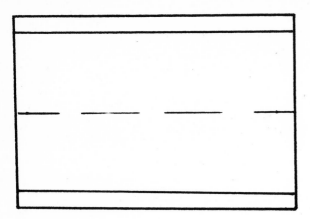

**49**    *Shape of welt or flap*

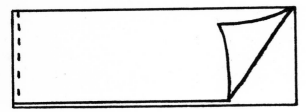

**49a**    *Flap folded in half ready for machining*

**49c and d**    *Designs showing welt and flap pockets*

**49b**    *As the flap appears on garment with corners reinforced*

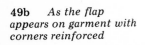

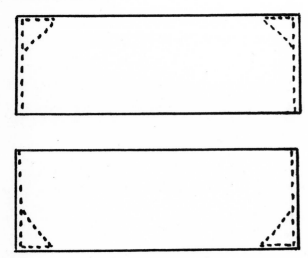

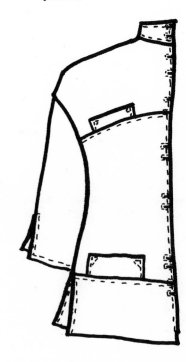

*Lined patch pocket*
Cut pocket to required size, plus 1 cm (½ in.) seam allowance, and
at the top of the pocket, approximately 4 cm (1½ in.).

Cut lining same size, but with only a seam allowance, and no facing,
along the top of the pocket (figure 48).

Place lining and pocket right side together, with the top seam
allowance on the lining folded down. Hold with paper clips.

Fold down the facing on the pocket, and hold with paper clips.

Machine round the pocket shape (figure 48a).

Turn pocket through slit in lining, and hand stitch lining onto
facing.

Hammer pocket edges to flatten.

Stitch onto garment as for unlined patch pocket (figure 48b).

*Welts and flaps*
These can be used together with patch pockets, pockets inserted in
seams, or by themselves to add design interest.

Cut skin twice the finished width of the flap or welt, plus two
seam allowances, and as long as the pocket opening (figure 49).

Fold flap in half and hammer along crease edge (figure 49a).

Stitch along the two short sides (figure 49b).

Attach onto garment by stitching along the long seam allowance.

Turn welts upwards, and flaps downwards.

Reinforce corners with extra stitching, or decorative studs (figure
49c).

# 2 Ideas for using small amounts of leather and suede in garments

A small area of leather or suede introduced into a garment is a way of making that garment look more expensive and exclusive, and also a way of learning how to work with skin before embarking on a major project.

One of the simplest ways to begin is with applied patches or inset pieces. These can be made from small skins, or off-cuts, and have great impact in a garment.

*Applied patches*
The position on the garment will dictate the size of the patch, but whatever the size, it is important to have a simple shape. Make a template for the patch. Not only will this make the cutting easier, but the template can be pinned onto the garment to test the effect before final application.

**50**   *Template shapes for patches*

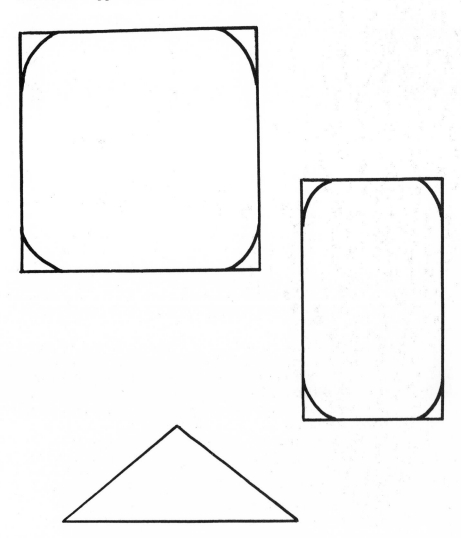

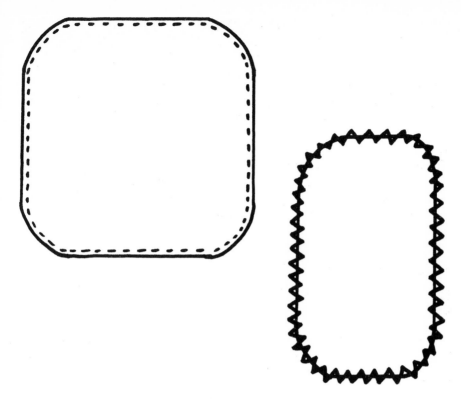

Trace round the template with a soft pencil or felt-tipped pen, on the wrong side of the skin. Cut out the shape with clean definite edges (figure 50).

51   *Patches can be applied with either straight or zigzag stitch*

Place double-sided *Sellotape* on the wrong side to hold the patch in position on the garment until it is finally stitched. If the patch is being applied as the garment is being made, the process is fairly simple. If, however, the pieces are being applied to cover worn areas in the garment, eg elbow or knee, it will be much easier to open the seams which are nearest to the patch position, so that they can be applied on a flat area.

If the patch is being sewn onto woven fabric, straight stitch is quite suitable. When sewing onto knitted fabric, a zigzag or stretch stitch is better. This will move in wear with the knitted fabric, and there will be less likelihood of tearing (figure 51).

This process has many variations. Patches can be turned into pockets by inserting a zip, or simply leaving the top edge unsewn. They can cover worn areas and make a feature from a necessity, reinforce areas of wear or stress, or be purely decorative (figure 52). They are suitable for both adults and children. Using skin with other fabrics presents few problems to modern dry cleaners. It is possible to buy washable leathers and suedes which are ideal for use on sweaters, etc. Chamois leather can also be used quite successfully in this way.

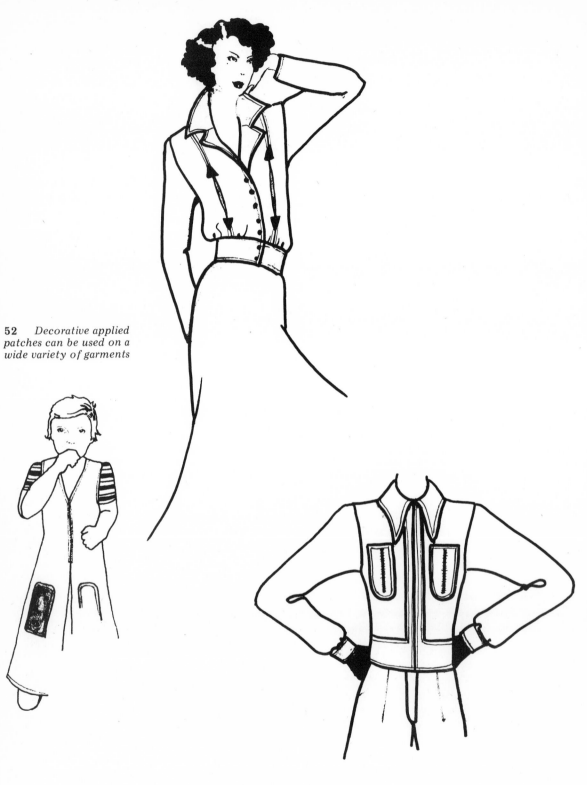

**52**    *Decorative applied
patches can be used on a
wide variety of garments*

**53**    *Inset pieces of skin are most effective when added as part of the design*

*Inset pieces*

These are a logical progression from patches. The pieces may take the form of yokes, straight or shaped bands, shoulder pieces, etc. They can either be a part of the existing design, yokes, etc, or new areas can be drawn onto a basic pattern, transferred onto the skin, and inserted into the garment (figure 53). Simple shapes are the easiest and most effective (figure 54).

Cut the insets to be made in skin, from the pattern shapes, remembering to add 1 cm (½ in. approx.) for turnings. The garment can then be made in the normal way using appropriate techniques of handling skin wherever necessary.

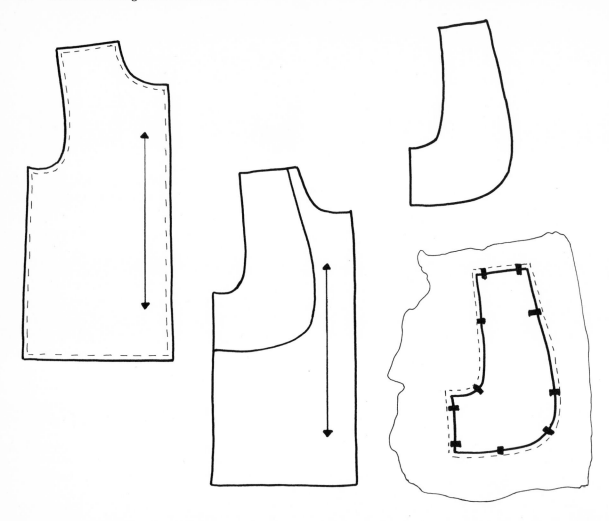

54    *Armhole yoke drawn onto a basic pattern and cut out in skin*

*Bindings*

Another simple way of introducing leather or suede into a garment is to use it as a binding. Front edges of jackets or coats, sleeves, necklines, pocket edges are all areas where skin bindings are effective (figure 55).

This trimming can be applied in several ways depending on the style of garment, the type of fabric which the skin will be trimming, and the occasion when the garment will be worn.

If the garment is casual, made perhaps from flannel, knobbly tweed, double-sided cloth, the following methods could be used:

Cut strips of skin twice the finished width of the binding and as long as required length. If a join has to be made in the length, use the skiving and glue method.

Fold the strip in half lengthwise, and press lightly, using brown paper and a warm iron(figure 56).

Place creased fold along the raw edge of the area being bound so that the skin lies equally on the upper and under side (figure 56a).

Machine from the right side through the top binding, the garment and the under binding, securing all layers with one row of machining. Further rows of machining may be added for decoration. The stitching may be matching or contrasting, or it could be stab-stitched by hand.

A more sophisticated result is achieved by the following method:

Cut binding strips as for previous method, adding 1 cm (½ in. approx.) to twice finished width.

Apply the right side of binding to the right side of garment, and machine through binding and garment (figure 57).

**55**  *Bindings can be used on many types of garments*

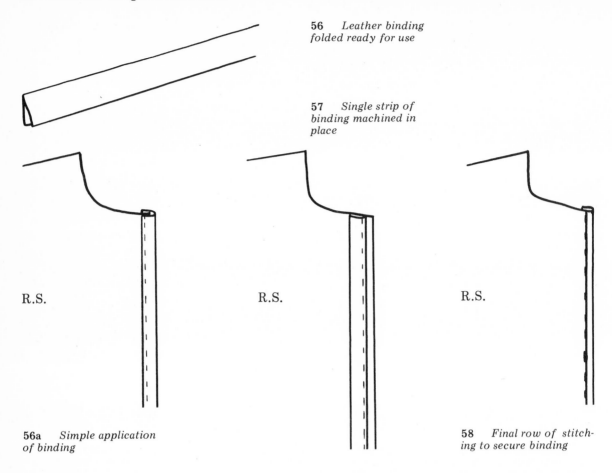

56    *Leather binding folded ready for use*

57    *Single strip of binding machined in place*

R.S.            R.S.            R.S.

56a    *Simple application of binding*

58    *Final row of stitching to secure binding*

Fold skin over garment edge so that it lies smoothly and evenly along the edge.

Machine from the right side through the 'crack' of the first seam, taking care to catch in the skin on the underside of the garment (figure 58).

*Braids*

Applying braids made from suede and leather is perhaps the most effective method of all to introduce this material into a garment, (figure 59).

A flat braid can be made simply by cutting the skin in strips of varying width and applying onto garments. This is particularly effective when used to emphasize a seam or style line. Usually the strips are sewn into position as the garment is being made. Narrow strips 1 - 2.5 cm (½ in. - 1 in. approx.) are most effective if left plain and machined onto the garment with either matching or contrasting thread.

Wider strips 2.5 - 3.5 cm (1 in. - 1½ in. approx.) are suitable for further decoration.

Machine embroidery produces a highly decorative effect, and can be worked in matching, contrasting, or lurex threads depending on the design and fabric. Patterns can also be punched in wider braid. This produces a much lighter effect on the garment, and can be used with crêpe, chiffon, and satin, in addition to fabrics more usually associated with leather and suede.

Soft-leather thonging, or narrow strips of suede can be plaited and knotted to produce attractive braids. These can be made of one colour, or of subdued tones to produce a sophisticated effect, or of brighter colours for sports wear or children's clothes.

Stitch the thongs to a small piece of fabric to stabilize them before starting to plait. This fabric can then be pinned down onto a board, and provide the tension for a good rhythm when plaiting.

When complete, stitch again close to the top and bottom length of braid, and cut away the starting fabric.

Apply the braid by hand, stitching behind the plait loops.

59   *Selection of braids made from suede and leather*

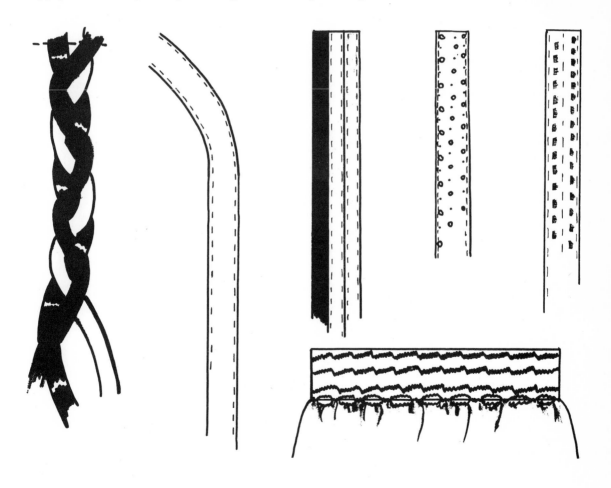

**60**    *Straps used as a decorative feature*

*Straps*
These are a development from the wider flat braid. The width of the strap will be decided by its position and function on the garment (figure 60).

If undecided about the width and shape of the straps, cut out several variations in paper and pin in position on the garment to check the effect, before cutting out the skin.

If the strap is to form a fastening it will be more serviceable if the section which is to be threaded through the buckle is cut double.

Stitch a single strap into position, cut another piece of leather the same shape as that part of the strap which is left free.

Glue the two together.

When the glue is dry, top stitch for extra strength.

*Pockets*
These are a very obvious design area for the use of skin. All the standard pockets — patch, welt, flap, bound — can be made effectively in skin using the normal methods of construction, and specialized techniques where necessary.

Reduce bulk wherever possible by skiving or trimming.

*Collars*
These are good places to use skin but the choice of design is important as leather often 'crocks' in this position, and suede becomes marked on the collar crease fairly quickly. The tailored collar and rever is quite difficult to achieve with a degree of professionalism, and unless one is experienced it might be wiser to choose another style of collar.

'Flat' and 'roll' collars are easier to manage, and yet offer variety of style. These collars can be made in the normal way, but, in most cases, interfacing will not be necessary if the entire collar, upper and under collar, are made in skin. If the under collar is made in fabric, and the top collar in skin, then interfacing will probably improve the finished result. It will depend on the weight of fabric and the type of skin.

Collars can also be made detachable, especially if the main garment is likely to be washed frequently. The collar is completed and then mounted onto tape. Sew press-studs onto tape and neckline of the garment for simple attachment (figure 61).

In all designs, top-stitching will help to flatten the collar edge and produce a crisp, definite shape.

*Cuffs*
In many designs where the collar is made from skin, the cuffs are also, and these become the prominent features of the garment (figure 62).

Normal methods of construction are used with the special techniques for skin, where needed.

Lining the cuffs with matching fabric or lining material, and trim-

**62**    *Detachable collar attached with press-studs*

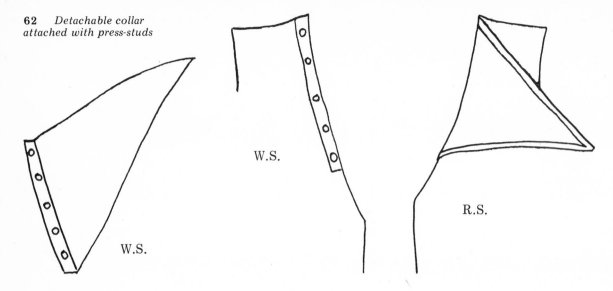

W.S.

W.S.

R.S.

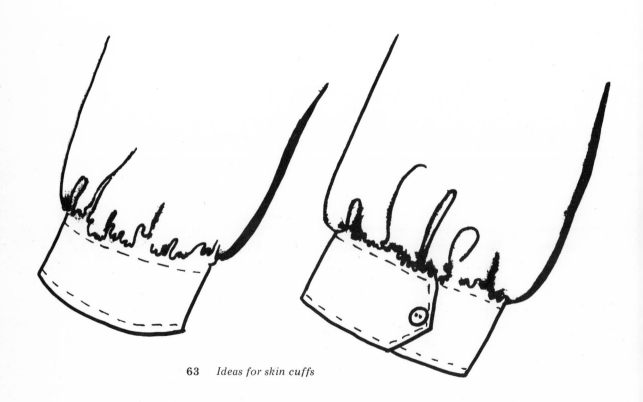

**63**    *Ideas for skin cuffs*

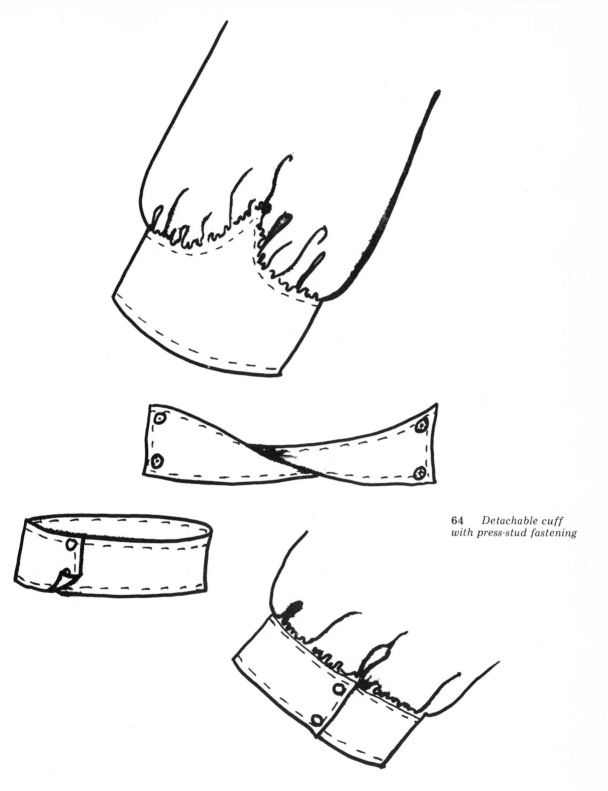

64    *Detachable cuff
with press-stud fastening*

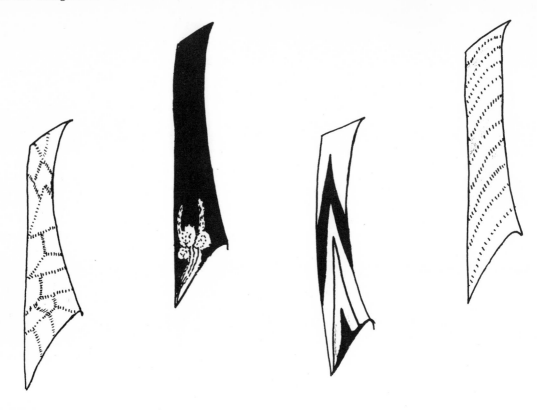

61    *Ideas for decorative treatment of collars*

ming the inside seams helps to keep the outline of the cuffs sharp and definite. Top-stitching flattens edges and provides a trimming. Interesting detachable cuffs can be made which are particularly useful if the garment is washable.

Take a paper pattern from the cuff shape of the garment and add 2 cm (¾ in. approx.) for turning to underarm seam.

Cut out this shape in skin. If the cuff is to be faced the lining is also cut from this pattern.

Apply any surface decoration to the cuff, eg appliqué, embroidery, etc.

Stitch *Velcro* onto 2 cm (¾ in.) underarm seam.

Slip cuff in position when garment is on the figure, and secure *Velcro* fastening. Press studs could be used as an alternative fastening. The cuffs could also be attached to the garment with press-studs (figure 63).

The idea of detachable collar and cuffs offer many variations. Because it is a small area, quite elaborate treatment that might be too complicated for a whole garment, could be used. Small patch-work, lattice strips, machine or hand embroidery, appliqué, beading, tucking, thonging, are all effective, and can give quality to an other-wise simple garment (figure 64).

*Note on cleaning*
Specialist cleaning is recommended for a garment made entirely in suede or leather.

Although this is fairly expensive a reputable cleaner will spend time and skill restoring the garment to its original shape and colour.

If suede or leather is used with another fabric, the method of cleaning suitable for the main fabric should be used, eg if a wool tweed coat had a suede shoulder yoke, it could be cleaned by a normal dry cleaning fluid and no specialist treatment would normally be necessary. However, there is sometimes a danger of colour from suede 'leaking', so, if the suede were of a very strong contrast to the main garment, eg burgundy suede on pink wool, specialist treatment might be needed in that case.

When skin is used with a fabric which is normally washed, ie cotton, synthetics, knitteds, careful treatment is needed. If the skin is washable, then there is no problem — wash the garment by hand to suit the main fabric. If the skin is not marked as washable and you are uncertain about washing the garment, the following method can be used:

> Wash the garment with a liquid soap cleanser or soap flakes in water comfortably hot. If the garment is especially dirty, eg children's wear, these areas could be washed first with a stronger detergent, but keep detergent away from the skin and rinse well.

> Rinse the garment and spin lightly, pull the skin areas into shape by hand.

> Dry out of doors if possible, away from direct heat, which would harden the skin.

> Iron garment in the usual way, pressing the skin areas through layers of brown paper.

*Author's note*    I have washed woollen sweaters with elbow patches, cotton jackets with inset pieces, and toddlers' jeans with knee patches in this way, with no great mishap — but the decision is yours!

# 3 Accessories

Good quality, original accessories are a great asset in producing a well-dressed appearance. However, they are often very expensive to buy and sometimes not readily available in local stores and shops.

Small pieces of skin can be made into interesting, attractive belts, handbags, and other accessories which will bring quality and originality to existing clothes, and give years of wear and satisfaction (figure 65).

## BELTS

The simplest type of belt is straight in shape, approximately 2.5 cm (1 in.) wide, with an attractive fastening. It can be unlined or backed with soft or strong material, depending on the weight of the skin and the degree of firmness required in the finished belt. This style of belt suits most figure-types and is endlessly useful.

Small pieces of skin can be joined together in a decorative way to produce the long length needed for a belt. Suede, leather, canvas and other fabrics can also be combined to produce attractive belts (figure 66).

**Simple straight belt**
*Stage 1*    Cut out the belt from pattern (see pattern one on page 108).
*Stage 2*    If the belt has to be pieced, arrange the joins to give a pleasing effect.

**65**  *Ideas for piecing belts with a variety of materials*

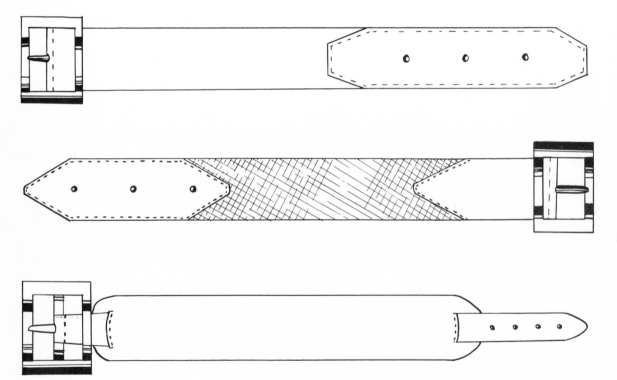

*Stage 3*    Thread the buckle through the straight end, and fasten back the tab, either by stitching or a metal stud.

*Stage 4*    If the buckle has a prong, punch holes, placing the first one at the normal waist measurement, then at 1 cm (½ in. approx.) intervals.

*Stage 5*    Additional rows of stitching in matching or contrasting thread, give a professional finish.

*Stage 6*    This type of unlined belt can be made in many widths and weights of skin

**Straight belt with petersham stiffening**    Method 1 (see pattern I)

*Stage 1*    Cut out the belt using the paper pattern (see p. 108) as guide. If the belt has to be pieced, arrange the joins to give an attractive pleasing effect.

*Stage 2*    Cut a length of toning petersham, omitting the buckle extension section. Trim the petersham to match the shaped end of the belt.

*Stage 3*    Machine the petersham to the skin, following the shape of the outer edge of the belt.

*Stage 4*    Thread buckle through the unstiffened end, and sew back the tab.

66    *Variety of straight unlined belts*

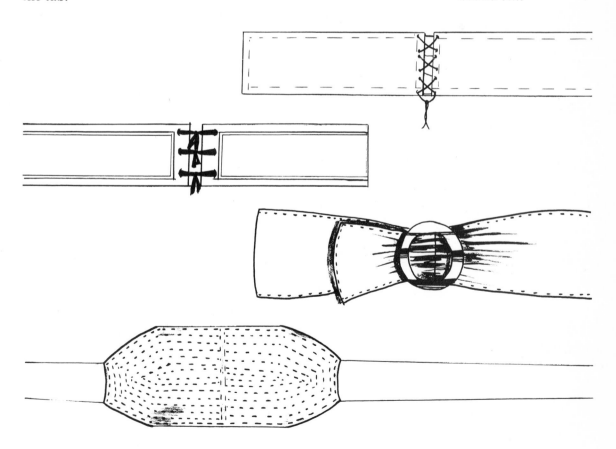

*Stage 5*    If the buckle has a prong, punch metal eyelets in position, placing the first eyelet at the normal waist measurement, and then at 1 cm (½ in.) intervals.

Further rows of stitching can be added, and stab-stitching by hand, using heavy thread, is very effective.

**Straight belt with petersham stiffening**    Method 2 (see pattern I)
This is similar to the previous method and is especially suitable for the softer skins.

*Stage 1*    Cut out the belt using the paper pattern (see p. 108) as guide, allowing 2 cm (¾ in. approximately) turnings all round. Arrange piecing if necessary.

*Stage 2*    Cut a length of toning petersham, omitting the buckle extension section. Trim the petersham to match the shaped end of the belt.

*Stage 3*    Place the petersham down the centre of the belt, and hold in position with double sided *Sellotape*. Glue turnings and press down onto the petersham. Hammer edges (figure 67).

**67**    *Petersham stiffening in place with ends shaped*

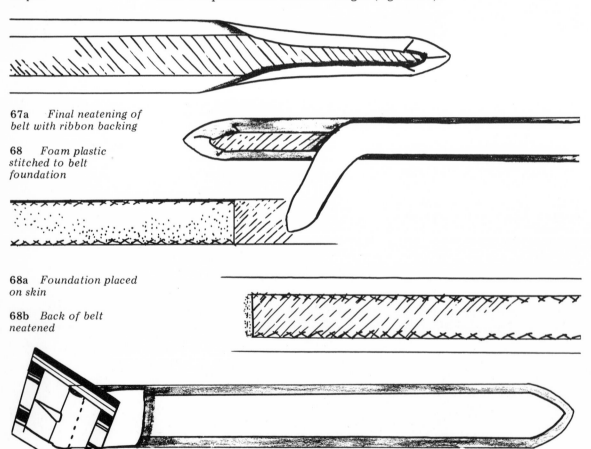

**67a**    *Final neatening of belt with ribbon backing*

**68**    *Foam plastic stitched to belt foundation*

**68a**    *Foundation placed on skin*

**68b**    *Back of belt neatened*

*Stage 4*   Line the back of the belt with petersham ribbon, glue in position (figure 67a).
*Stage 5*   Finish off as for previous method.

**Straight belt, using padding and leather backing** (pattern I)
*Stage 1*   Cut out the entire belt shape in foundation material. This can be stiffened petersham or heavy weight vilene.
*Stage 2*   Cut out a length of foam plastic, 6 - 10 mm (¼ in. to 3/8 in.) approximately in thickness, omitting buckle extension. Place onto the belt foundation material (figure 68).
*Stage 3*   Machine the two materials together round the outer edges.
*Stage 4*   Select the skin to be used for covering this foundation. A thin lightweight skin gives the best result; reptile skin is particularly effective.
*Stage 5*   Cut the skin from the belt pattern, adding 1 cm (½ in. approx.) all round. Piece if necessary.
*Stage 6*   Place the skin over the foundation, with the padded section immediately under the skin; fold turnings onto the underside of the foundation, and glue into position (figure 68a).
*Stage 7*   Thread the buckle through the unpadded buckle extension and fasten back tab.
*Stage 8*   Cut a length of thin skin, or toning ribbon, and stick onto the back of the belt to neaten (figure 68b). Punch eyelets if needed. This belt has a slightly rounded look.

Belts over 5 cm (2 in.) wide fit better and are more comfortable in wear if they are shaped. The following pattern for a contoured belt fits well down into the waist curve.

**Contoured belt** (pattern 1)
*Stage 1*   Cut contoured shape from stiffening material, omitting buckle extension.
*Stage 2*   Cut this shape out again in the lining fabric, adding 1 cm (½ in.) turnings all round.
*Stage 3*   Place the foundation shape on the wrong side of lining, fold turnings over onto foundation and machine all round the edge (figure 69).
*Stage 4*   Cut entire belt shape from skin. Because this belt is fairly wide it gives greater scope for featured joins and decoration, and these should be done at this stage.
*Stage 5*   Place the covered foundation shape, and the skin shape wrong sides together. Hold in position with double-sided *Sellotape.*
*Stage 6*   Machine together round the entire belt shape.
*Stage 7*   Thread buckle through unstiffened end and fasten back the tab. Punch eyelets if necessary (figure 69a).
This contoured belt can also be made unlined using medium to heavy weight skin.

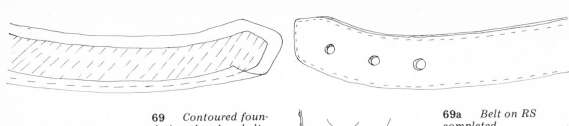

**69** *Contoured foundation placed on belt shape with one side turned up in final position*

**69a** *Belt on RS completed*

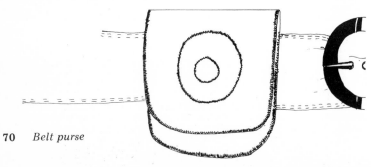

**70** *Belt purse*

**70a** *Slits in back of purse to allow belt to pass through*

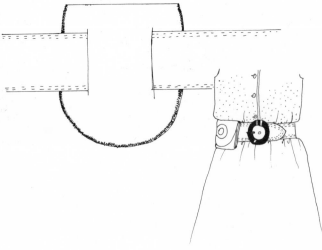

These methods can be adapted to provide a variety of designs to suit all types of clothes and occasions.

Belts can be fastened with: lacings, clasps, buttons, studs, tabs, and many other types of haberdashery, in addition to the traditional buckle.

**Belt Purse** (pattern 1)

A purse to slip onto a belt is a useful accessory. This is a simple design made from two small pieces of suede (figure 70).

*Stage 1*    Trace off the pattern shapes onto skin.

*Stage 2*    Apply decoration to the purse flap.

*Stage 3*    Sew main pieces and gusset together. Match points X.

*Stage 4*    Slash two slits in the back of the purse to allow the belt to pass through (figure 70a).

*Stage 5*    Apply small pieces of *Velcro* for fastening.

1    For belts see pages 66 to 69 and 108
     For bag see pages 74, 75 and 109

**2**   See pages 76, 77 and 109

## HANDBAGS

A real leather handbag is often thought of as a great luxury, but with patience and care, it is within the skill of most people who sew, and need not cost a fortune. A classic leather bag will give years of wear, and a pretty suede pouch makes a glamorous addition to an evening outfit.

Handicraft and specialist shops usually have a selection of frames, whilst jumble sales, charity and junk shops are often a source of old handbags with attractive frames which are re-usable.

The shape and style of the frame will dictate the shape and size of the finished bag. Make paper patterns of several different shapes and try them with the frame to visualize the finished effect. If more than one colour of skin is to be used, this too can be planned on the paper shape, and then used as a pattern for cutting the sections.

**Rod frame** (pattern 2)

This type of frame is very simple and easy to manage. The handbag illustrated was made in brown calf leather with toning stitched decoration, on a 22.5 cm (9 in.) frame (figure 73).

*Stage 1*    Make a paper pattern for the handbag and gusset, trace round these shapes on the wrong side of the skin, adding small turnings. Cut out.

*Stage 2*    Cut out the same shapes in lining material.

*Stage 3*    Apply any stitched decoration at this stage.

*Stage 4*    Assemble the handbag and gusset using a plain seam. Match points at X.

*Stage 5*    Repeat this process in the lining material.

*Stage 6*    Slip the lining inside handbag wrong side lining to wrong side skin, turn over from the right side along dotted line, and stitch in position. This neatens the lining and provides the channel for the rod in one process. Neaten the lining at the top of the gusset by hand-stitching.

*Stage 7*    Slip the metal rod of frame through the channel and screw in position.

*Stage 8*    If the handle of the frame is not to your liking, you can replace it by a leather one using the existing loops, as in the example shown.

**71**    *Rod frame with suggested shapes*

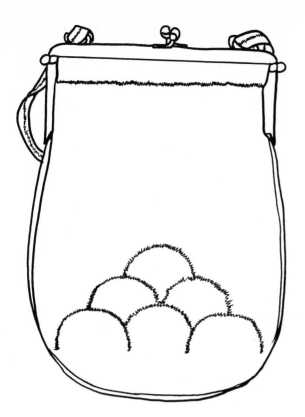

**73    Rod frame handbag in brown leather**

**72    Clasp frame with shapes**

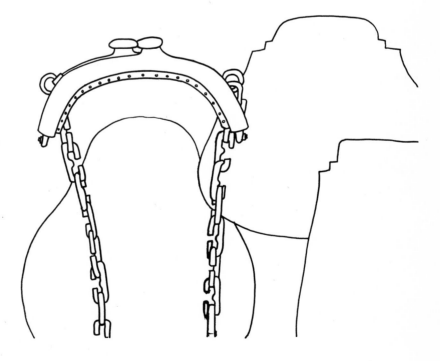

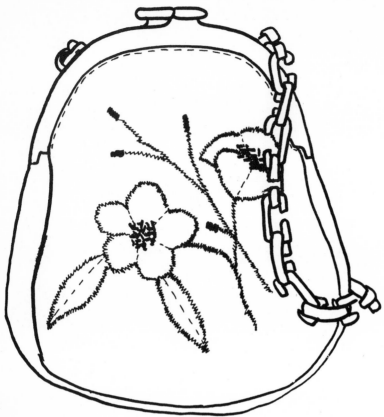

**74**   *Clasp frame hand-bag in pink suede*

**Clasp frame** (pattern 2)
Frames of this type usually have small holes punched in them to enable the handbag to be sewn on by hand. The illustrated handbag (figure 74) was made in pink suede with fabric appliqué and beaded trimming. Proceed as for rod frame handbag up to stage 5.

*Stage 6*   Slip the lining inside the handbag wrong side to wrong side. Stitch the two together round the top of the shape. Zigzag stitch was used to give a neat finish.

*Stage 7*   Attach the handbag to the frame by hand. As both these stitching processes are visible in the finished bag, they should be made as decorative as possible, perhaps by using contrasting or heavy thread.

**Ring handles** (pattern 3)
This type of handle is very simple and one of the most effective and ideal if you are using fabric and skin together. The rings can be found in plain or stained wood, plastic, and on older bags, bone and ivory.

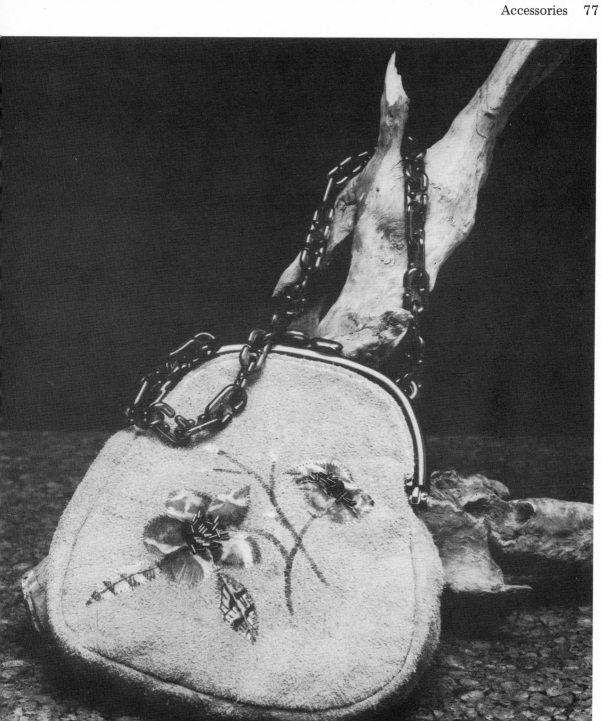

The illustrated bag (figure 75) was made from brown corduroy, suede and leather.

*Stage 1*    Cut out two handbag shapes in corduroy, and two in lining fabric.

*Stage 2*    Trace off the shapes to be cut in skin. (In our example, the lower piece was brown leather, the upper section a lighter brown suede and an additional narrow strip in beige suede was cut to cover the join of these two sections).

*Stage 3*    Stitch the skin shapes onto one of the corduroy sections.

*Stage 4*    Machine the two corduroy pieces together right side to right side from X to X. Repeat the process in the lining fabric.

*Stage 5*    Place the lining inside handbag, wrong side to wrong side and turn in small turnings on both handbag and lining from Z to Z and Y to Y, and machine from the right side. Neaten the top edge in a similar manner.

*Stage 6*    Thread the top edge through the ring handles, fold on dotted line and stitch in position.

This same method can be used with wooden 'knitting bag' handles, although the shape of the handbag would be slightly different in order to accommodate the extra width in this type of handle (figure 76).

**75**    *Ring-handled bag in corduroy, suede and leather*

**76**    *Knitted bag handles used for handbag*

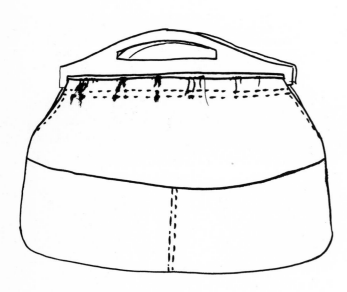

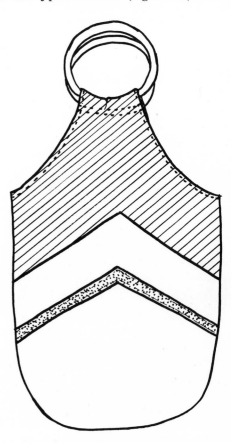

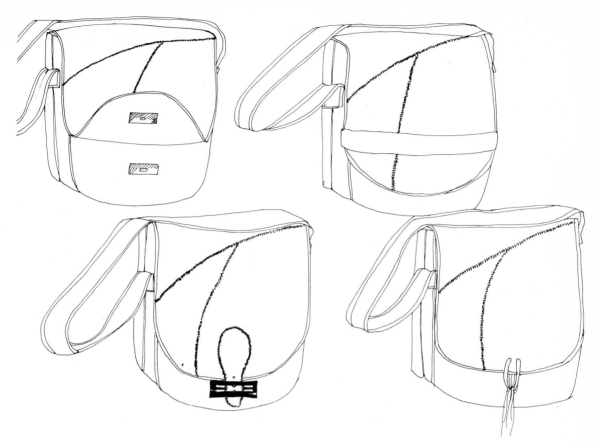

**Shoulder bag** (pattern 4)

This is a popular type of handbag that can be made with many variations to suit the type of skin used.

The illustrated handbag (figure 77) was made in random patchwork from skins of russet, brown and gold.

*Stage 1*    Trace the handbag shapes onto heavyweight *Vilene*, the gusset and strap shapes onto skin.

*Stage 2*    Cut the skin in random shapes, and place on the handbag foundation, holding in position with double-sided adhesive tape. Plan the whole area before you begin to stitch; this will ensure a balanced distribution of colour and texture.

*Stage 3*    Stitch the skin onto the foundation. This can be done by straight, or zigzag machining, or by hand, using stab-stitch.

*Stage 4*    Cut out the handbag shapes in thin cotton wadding, and also in lining fabric. For the lining, choose a material that does not fray, or a thin skiver skin.

*Stage 5*    Trim the cotton wadding so that it is slightly smaller than the handbag shape. Hold in position on the shape with double-sided adhesive tape.

*Stage 6*    Place the lining in position over the cotton wadding and

**77**    *Shoulder bag made in random patchwork with a variety of fastenings*

**78**   *Suede hat trimmed with plaited leather and wooden beads*

**79**   *Six sectioned leather cap*

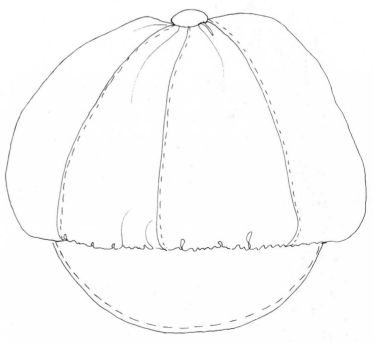

stitch round the edges onto the foundation. Trim the edges to a clean shape if necessary.

*Stage 7*    Sew the main sections of the handbag and gusset together, with a plain seam. Match X points. Neaten the top of the gusset by turning over approximately 2.5 cm (1 in.) of gusset and sticking it down on the inside.

*Stage 8*    Neaten the edges of the handbag flap with a binding of narrow leather.

*Stage 9*    Cut the shoulder strap to the required length and bind the edges with narrow leather strips. Attach to the handbag by heavy metal studs.

The fastening for this handbag can be an 'invisible' stud which can be bought from a specialist dealer, or it can be one of the methods illustrated.

The use of cotton wadding in this handbag produces a soft, 'squashy' appearance. The bag can, of course, be made without this padding.

## HATS (pattern 5)

Pale green suede was used for the hat in figure 78. The trimming was brown leather thonging, plaited, and the ends finished off with knots and wooden beads.

*Stage 1*    Trace the pattern shapes (if a shape is to be cut round more than once, this is indicated on the pattern) and mark onto the wrong side of the skin.

*Stage 2*    Assemble the crown by machining the sections together, with plain seams, starting at the crown point and working to the headline. Top-stitching along the seam-lines will produce a better shape and eliminate the need for pressing.

*Stage 3*    Join the centre back seams on the two brim shapes. Top-stitch and trim away the seam allowance.

*Stage 4*    Place the brim sections together, wrong side to wrong side round the outer edge. Several rows of stitching will stabilize the edge and produce a more professional finish.

*Stage 5*    Join the crown to brim with a plain seam.

*Stage 6*    Apply trimming. A button shape can be covered and stitched to the crown point.

The hat can be lined. Machine crown sections together, press, and attach by hand round the headline. This will also neaten the headline seam.

If the skin is very soft, the hat will be improved if *Vilene* is used for interfacing.

## CAP (pattern 6)

Use the same method as for the hat using the cap and peak sections (figure 79).

# 4  Decoration

Because skin comes in many weights and variations, and is a non-fraying material, it responds successfully to most forms of decoration.

## PATCHWORK

This is a very popular way of using skin; it is economical as well as decorative. Small pieces can be used for decoration and doing this is also a very good introduction to the use of suede and leather for the first time. Most classic patchwork shapes can be used as well as random patchwork: jerkins, skirts, bags, belts, hats, are all suitable products and can be made from the same basic method.

Make a foundation shape of the article or garment to be made, *vilene* is a good stable material to use, and can be bought in many grades to suit the varying weights of the skin. Fitting adjustments can be made on this foundation when garments are being made (figure 80).

Cut the skin into the desired shapes, either regular or random, and place on the foundation shape using double-sided adhesive tape (figure 81).

**80**   *Vilene foundation shape for patchwork skirt*

**81**   *Patchwork being assembled on skirt*

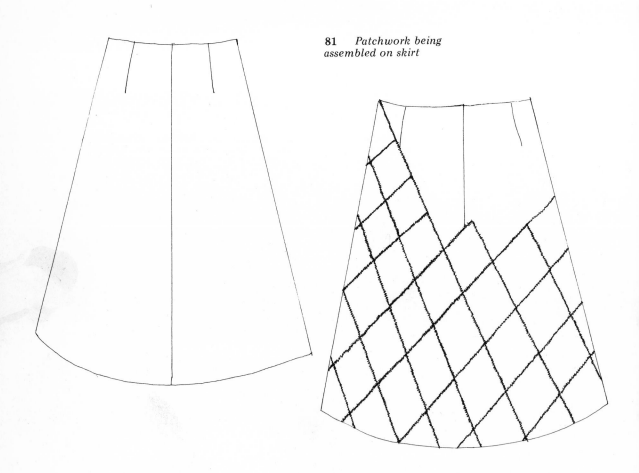

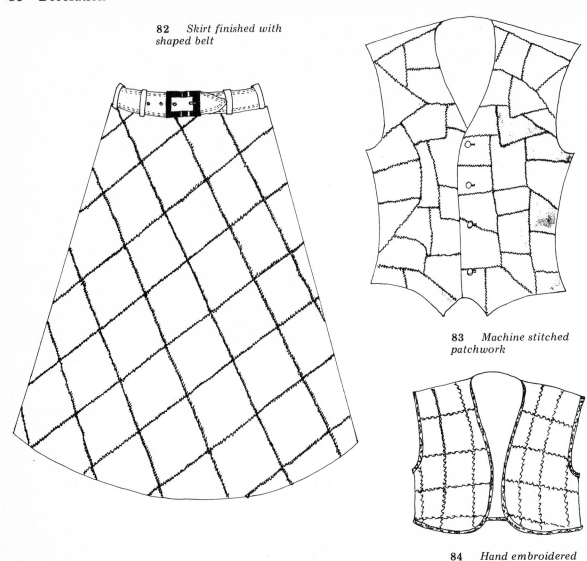

**82**    *Skirt finished with shaped belt*

**83**    *Machine stitched patchwork*

**84**    *Hand embroidered patchwork*

Plan a whole section before beginning to stitch. By using adhesive tape, patches can be moved about until a pleasing balance of colour and texture is achieved (figure 82).

Stitch the patches in position onto the foundation shape. Zigzag machine stitching is both quick and effective (figure 83). Hand-stitching obviously takes longer, but embroidery stitches in heavy thread produce an attractive peasant effect and are well worth the effort if only a small article is being planned (figure 84).

When the patchwork has been stitched onto the foundation, complete the garment using relevant skin techniques where necessary.

## APPLIQUÉ

Cutting out and applying attractive patterns or 'motifs' in leather or suede (known as appliqué) can be the striking feature of any new garment, whether bought or made.

Leather can be applied to suede, and suede to leather, and both can be used with other fabrics to produce a formal or informal effect.

Simple shapes are the most effective and the easiest to execute. Additional detail can be provided by beading and embroidery. Always make a template of the shape from thin card.

The method of working appliqué using suede and leather, is an extension of the applied patch process already given.

## BEADING

The beadwork used by American Indians on skin is well known, and a more detailed look at this type of work will provide many ideas for decoration. However, there is such a variety of beads available nowadays, that even the complete beginner can produce effective beading quite successfully (figure 85).

Small glass beads can be packed closely together or used with other methods of decoration, eg as centres in appliqué flowers, or to outline a featured seam. A long, thin beading needle is necessary with this type of bead.

Beads of wood, glass and metal produce entirely different effects, and are most attractive when used with heavy embroidery on peasant and ethnic clothes and accessories.

## EMBROIDERY

This is perhaps most effective when used with an other method of decoration, eg patchwork, appliqué, beading. Strong, bold stitching and colour is most suitable for skin, whether done by machine or hand.

Machine embroidery usually produces a formal, elegant result and is therefore very suitable for evening wear and garments made from fine, lightweight skins (figure 86).

Hand embroidery is highly decorative, lovely for sports clothes, casual clothes and accessories, and also for informal evening wear.

## TUCKS AND GATHERS

Both these methods of controlling fullness can be used with fine lightweight skins.

*Tucks* are particularly effective and can be in varying widths, from pin-tucks, covering an entire yoke or cuff, to wider 2.5 cm (1 in.) tucks producing either fullness or decoration (figure 87).

**85** *Ideas for beading on skin*

**86**  *Embroidery used
to give an ethnic look to
suede and leather*

**87** *Tucks and gathers*

*Gathers* are used in small areas because of the difficulty in pressing, eg gathered into a yoke or cuff. They can also be controlled by simple smocking stitches.

## QUILTING

English, Italian and Trapunto quilting can all be used successfully with suede and leather.

Motifs using Italian and Trapunto quilting look very elegant on revers, yokes and pockets, while English quilting can be used in larger areas, eg on waistcoats; as inserted bands, skirt hems, etc.

### Shawl
This shawl (figure 88) was made from lightweight cream jersey, with two shades of pink suede for the flower; green machine embroidery, and shaded pearl beads.

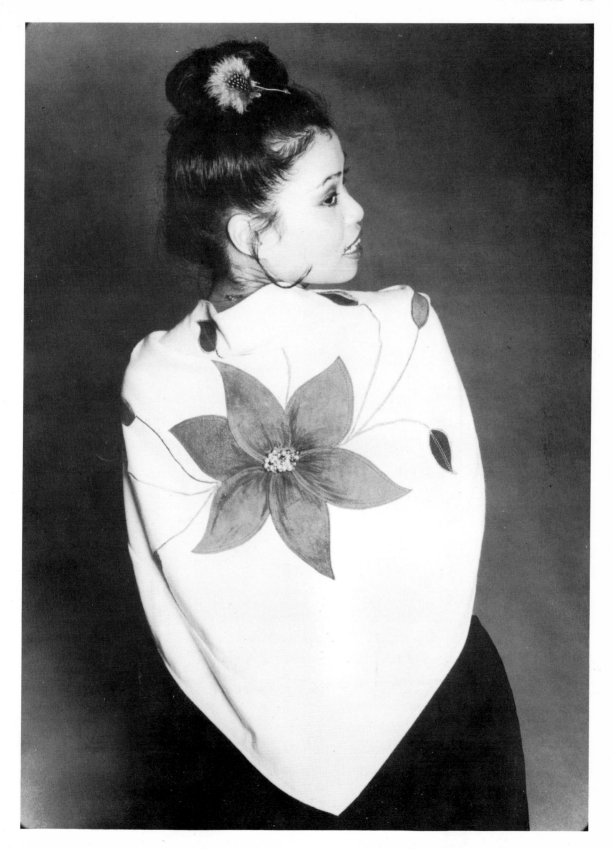

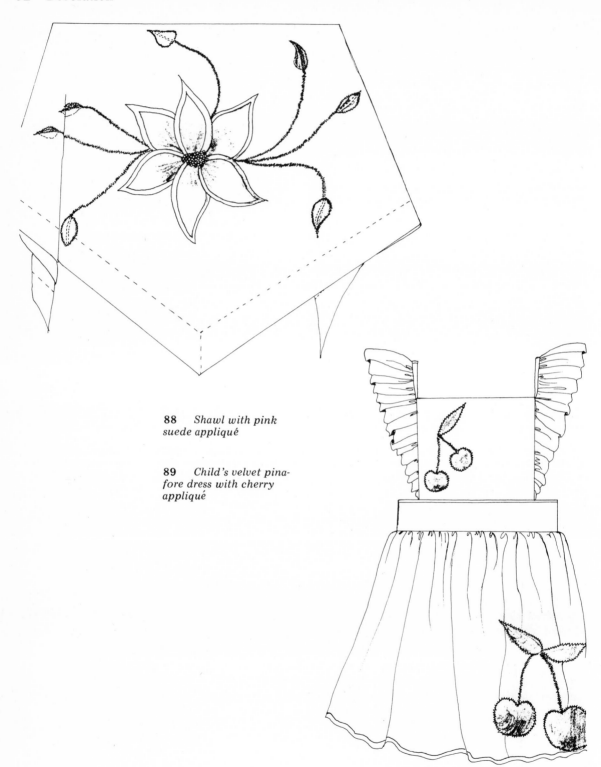

88 *Shawl with pink suede appliqué*

89 *Child's velvet pina-fore dress with cherry appliqué*

The size and shape of the shawl will be dictated by the width and length of the fabric used.

As the cream jersey was only 69 cm (27 in.) wide, a border was added. Also, because the jersey was lightweight, the shawl was made double, but the appliqué was worked on single fabric with a muslin backing to give stability.

*Stage 1*    Trace the petal shapes onto thin card to make a template (figure 97).
*Stage 2*    Using the template as a guide, cut out the suede pieces.
*Stage 3*    Place double-sided adhesive tape behind each large petal and position on fabric.
*Stage 4*    Machine round the edges of the suede petals. Straight or zigzag stitch can be used, or a hand embroidery stitch.
*Stage 5*    Draw stem lines, and machine embroider with green thread, using a close zigzag stitch.
*Stage 6*    Place small petals in position, and stitch round the outside edges. In the example shown in figure 88 stitching in light and dark shades of pink thread was added to give extra depth.
*Stage 7*    Sew beads in the centre of the large flower.
*Stage 8*    Add a border to the shawl, if desired. The edges can also be fringed.

**Child's blue velvet pinafore dress** — See colour plate facing page 96.
This simple cherry design in figure 89 is worked in the same method as the shawl. The motif could be extended all around the skirt, applied to a pocket, or worked on the bodice and repeated on the blouse in embroidery.

**Sweater**
Appliquéd motifs on knitwear are most attractive, and a simple way of making such garments individual and unusual (figure 90).

Back the area with muslin to stabilize the knitted fabric and prevent it from stretching when applying the motif.

**Man's waistcoat** (patterns 7 and 8)
In the example shown (figure 91) a fairly heavyweight beige leather was used. The skin was marked rather badly, but by careful cutting, the marked areas were placed in the front and centre back panels, and far from being a disadvantage, added to the rugged effect. Because of the weight of the skin, some of the seams were thonged together.
*Stage 1*    Trace off the pattern shapes onto the skin.
*Stage 2*    Join the panels to make front and back sections.
*Stage 3*    Mark positions and punch holes on shoulder seams, side seams, round arm holes, down the fronts and lower edges. The holes were punched approximately 1 cm (½ in.) apart.
*Stage 4*    Lace shoulder and side seams together with narrow thonging, taking care to finish off well by threading the ends of the thonging

90    *Ideas for knitwear*

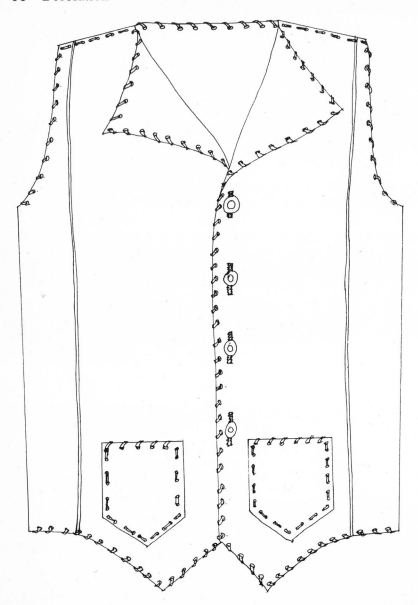

91    *Man's beige leather waistcoat*

back through a few holes at the seam endings.

*Stage 5*    Thong the front and lower edges, and the arm holes.

*Stage 6*    Machine-finished button holes were used for fastening in this example, but decorative studs could be an alternative method.

This waistcoat fits a 97 cm (38 in.) chest, but can be made larger by adding 2 cm (¾ in.) onto the side seams, and 1 cm (½ in. approx) onto the front edges.

To make the pattern smaller, deduct these measurements from the side seams and front edges.

3    See pages 92 and 93

4    *(Overleaf)* See pages 97, 98 and 115

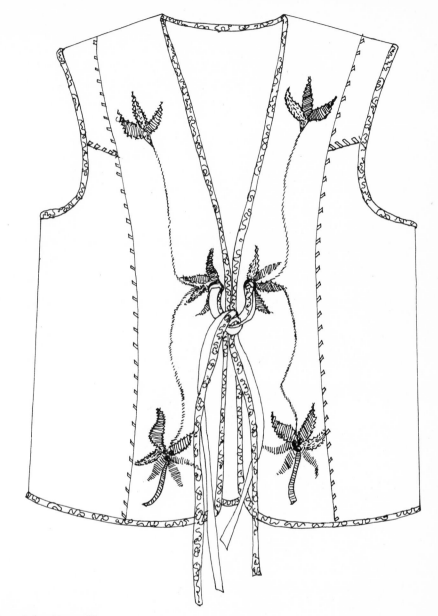

92    *Brown suede waist-coat, hand embroidered*

**Hand embroidered waistcoat (pattern 9)**
This garment was made from several shades of brown suede, with brown, rust, peach and green embroidery, wooden beads and floral cotton binding (figure 92).
*Stage 1*    Trace off the pattern shapes onto the skin.
*Stage 2*    Transfer the design onto the front panels. Use bold embroidery stitches with fairly heavy thread, and a glover's needle.
*Stage 3*    Sew the front panels together and oversew with embroidery thread.

*Stage 4*    Assemble the back sections, and then join shoulder and side seams. Top stitch all the seams to flatten them and give a good shape. A narrow strip of adhesive interfacing applied down the front and round the lower edge will prevent these areas stretching.

*Stage 5*    Cut out lining from the pattern and stitch together. Press.

*Stage 6*    Place the wrong side of lining to the wrong side of waistcoat and stitch together round the edges. This will hold the two materials together ready for binding. Stitch in similar manner round armholes.

*Stage 7*    Cut cross-way strips 2.5 cm (1 in.) wide from the binding fabric, and join together to make a long strip.

*Stage 8*    Apply the right side of the binding to the right side of the waistcoat and machine an even distance away from the edge all round the waistcoat. Machine in a similar way round the arm holes. Turn to inside of waistcoat and finish binding by hand.

*Stage 9*    Punch two holes and fix metal eyelets at point X on front. Make long ties from leather and binding fabric and thread through for fastening.

This pattern will fit a 92 cm (36 in.) bust.

To make it larger, add 2 cm (¾ in.) on side seams, and 1 cm (½ in. approx.) on the front edges.

To make it smaller, deduct these measurements from side seams and front edges.

### Machine embroidered waistcoat (pattern 10)

Golden-brown washable suede was used for this garment, with machine embroidery in pink, green and brown thread, using the automatic patterns on a swing-needle machine (figure 93).

*Stage 1*    Trace off the pattern shapes onto the wrong side of the skin.

*Stage 2*    If the suede is very soft, the front edges, armhole edges, and the entire peplum pieces, can all be stabilized by applying lightweight adhesive *Vilene*.

*Stage 3*    Machine darts in front bodice, cut dart open on the wrong side and press, using paper to protect the skin.

*Stage 4*    From right side, stitch two rows of machining in matching thread close to the dart line. This will flatten and 'set' the dart before applying the machine embroidery. If the skin is soft and lightweight, the dart turning can remain, to act as an additional foundation for the machine embroidery in this area, otherwise trim away turning. Machine embroider.

*Stage 5*    Join shoulder and side seams, and top-stitch in matching thread.

*Stage 6*    Machine embroider shoulder pieces. If these are to be lined, apply lining first and then embroider through suede and lining.

*Stage 7*    Attach shoulder pieces, right side to right side of waistcoat, matching points X and Y. Top-stitch round armhole, flattening seam and turning in lower armhole edge for neatening.

*Stage 8*    Machine front and back peplum sections together, and attach

**93**   *Gold suede waist-coat, machine embroidered*

**93a facing page**
*Pink washable suede evening blouse with machine embroidery and punched hole pattern*

to the lower edge of waistcoat. Top-stitch along this waistline seam.
*Stage 9*   If waistcoat is to be lined, assemble lining at this point and attach to waistcoat. Place the right side of the lining to the right side of the waistcoat, machine along front edges and round back neck line. Trim seam allowance, and top-stitch in matching thread from the right side to 'set' front edges. Turn under lower edge of lining, and attach to waistcoat at lower edge by top-stitching from the right side. Finish off by hand around arm holes.
*Stage 10*   Machine embroider front and lower edges, and back neckline.
*Stage 11*   Make ties and belt by cutting strips, 2.5 cm (1 in.) plus turnings, and applying machine embroidery. Make ties approximately 28 cm (11 in.) long, and attach to the waistcoat at Z.
*Stage 12*   Stitch hooks and eyes at waistline and behind ties.

**94**  *Cream chenille
sweater with appliqué
on a kangaroo pocket*

### Sweater (pattern 11)

This was a bought sweater in cream chenille. The kangaroo pocket was a similar fabric in sand colour, and the appliquéd pattern in small pieces of colourful suede and leather (figure 94).

*Stage 1*    Trace off the pocket shape and cut out twice in fabric and once in muslin. Trace off the appliqué shapes.

*Stage 2*    Tack muslin backing to one piece of fabric and apply skin appliqué. The smaller pieces are better stitched by hand.

*Stage 3*    Place pocket pieces right side together and machine along sides, curved pocket opening, and top edge. Trim seams and turn out through lower edge.

*Stage 4*    Tack out around machined edges and press to obtain a good shape.

*Stage 5*    Zigzag lower edge for neatening. Apply to sweater along the top edge of the sweater welt, the right side of the pocket to the right side of the sweater, and machine along edge.

*Stage 6*    Turn up the pocket into position on the sweater and top-stitch from the right side along the side seams, and top edge, leaving the curved sections for the pocket opening.

### Envelope Bag (pattern 12)

This very simple envelope bag was made in soft pink suede, trimmed with quilting, striped binding and wooden beads (figure 95).

*Stage 1*    Trace off the pattern shapes onto the wrong side of the skin.

*Stage 2*    Pad the flap sections of the bag with thin cotton wadding, holding it in position with double sided adhesive tape. Quilt this area with lines of straight or decorative machine stitches.

*Stage 3*    Cut lining sections. Place the wrong side of the lining to the wrong side of the bag, and machine together round outer edges.

*Stage 4*    Place front and back sections of the bag together, matching points X. Apply crossway strip, the right side of strip to the right side of the bag, and machine through the three layers, continuing round the flap shape.

*Stage 5*    Turn crossway strip over the raw edge and stitch by hand.

*Stage 6*    Make loop fastening from crossway strip and stitch in place. Attach toggle by a strip of the binding.

*Stage 7*    Cut length of suede for the handle. Fringe the ends by making clean slits the required length. Finish off the 'fringe' with wooden beads.

*Stage 8*    Attach this strap to the handbag by hand, and cover the stitches with wooden beads.

### Evening bag (pattern 12)

An attractive evening bag can be made from the same pattern as the envelope bag, using, perhaps, gold kid and Italian quilting and omitting the long strap handle (figure 96).

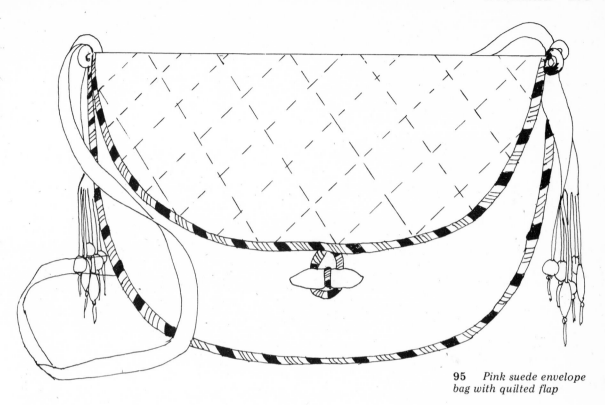

**95**   *Pink suede envelope bag with quilted flap*

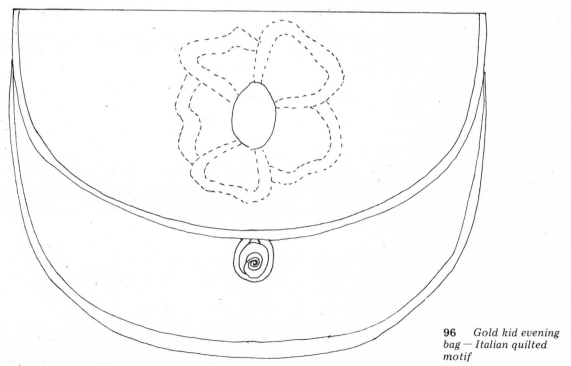

**96**   *Gold kid evening bag — Italian quilted motif*

**97**    *Waistcoat and shawl motifs*

**98**    *Sweater motifs*

**99**    *Cherry motif for child's pinafore dress*

# 5 Patterns

Transfer all patterns onto 1 cm squared paper for correct size.

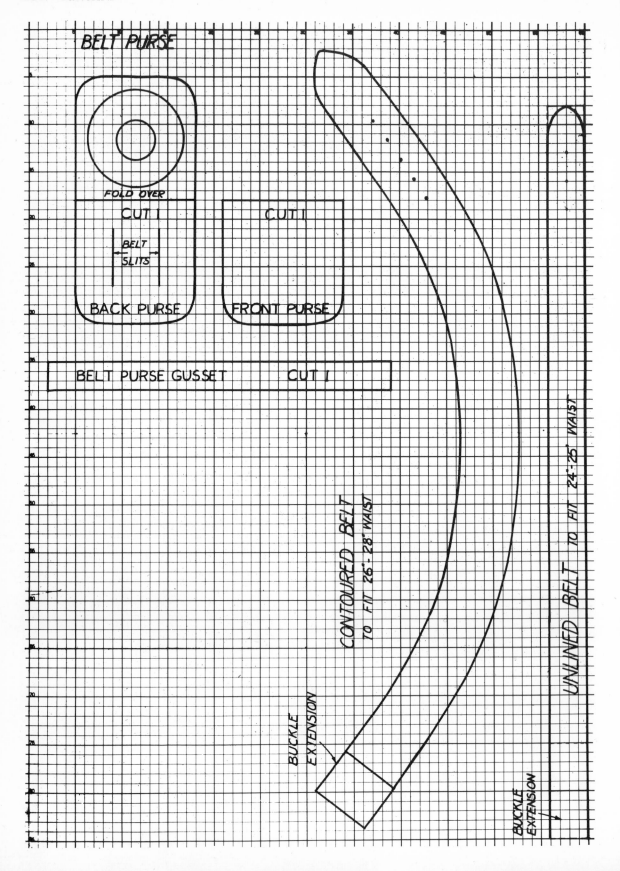

BELT PURSE

FOLD OVER

CUT 1

CUT 1

BELT SLITS

BACK PURSE

FRONT PURSE

BELT PURSE GUSSET    CUT 1

CONTOURED BELT

TO FIT 26"-28" WAIST

BUCKLE EXTENSION

UNLINED BELT TO FIT 24"-25" WAIST

BUCKLE EXTENSION

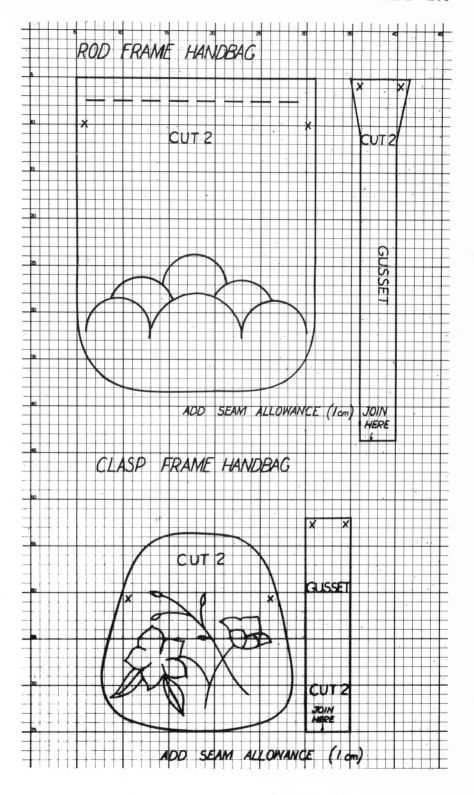

ROD FRAME HANDBAG

CUT 2

CUT 2

GUSSET

ADD SEAM ALLOWANCE (1cm) JOIN HERE

CLASP FRAME HANDBAG

CUT 2

GUSSET

CUT 2

JOIN HERE

ADD SEAM ALLOWANCE (1cm)

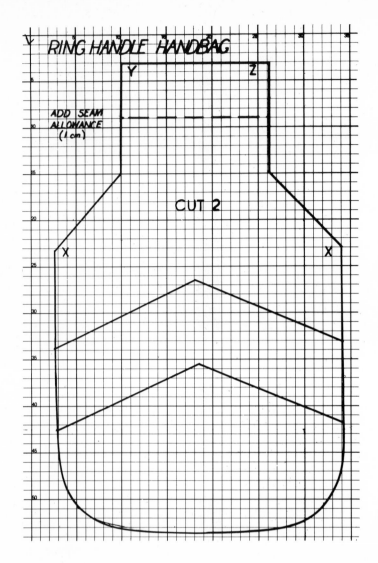

RING HANDLE HANDBAG

Y          Z

ADD SEAM
ALLOWANCE
(1 cm)

CUT 2

X                              X

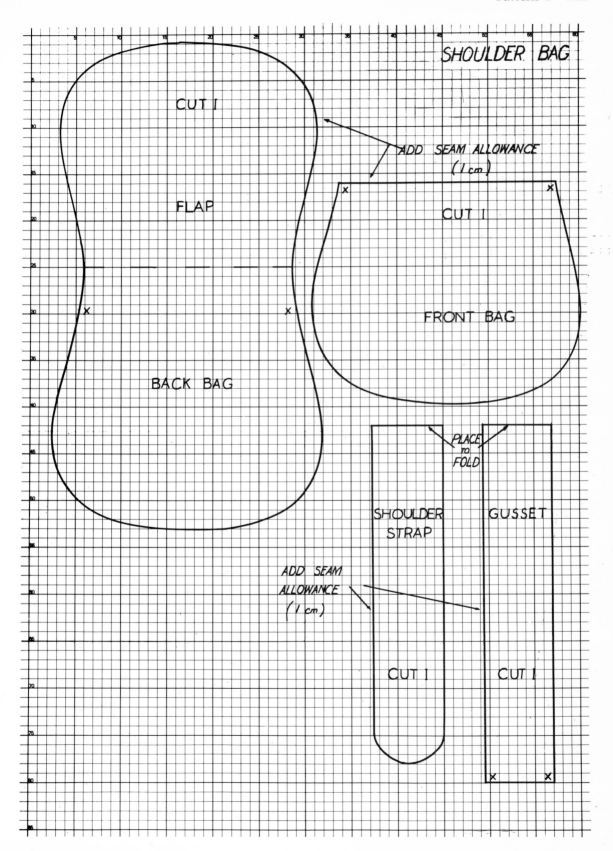

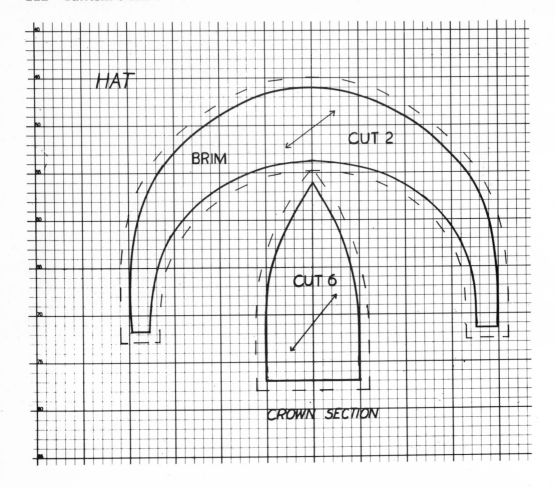

HAT

BRIM

CUT 2

CUT 6

CROWN SECTION

Pattern 6

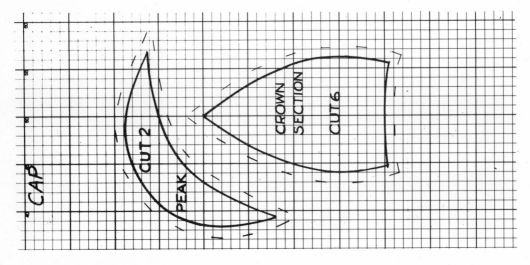

CAP

CUT 2

PEAK

CROWN SECTION

CUT 6

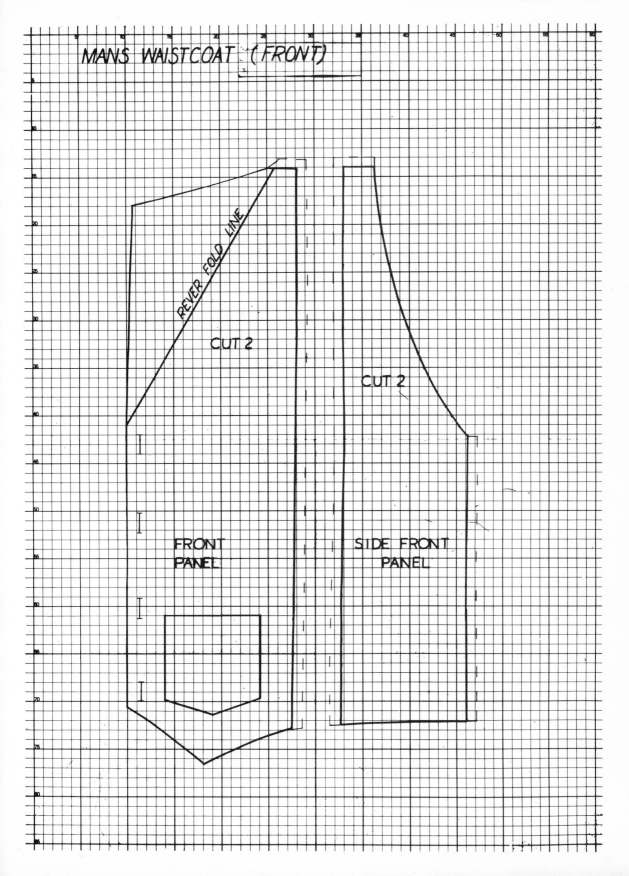

MANS WAISTCOAT (FRONT)

REVER FOLD LINE

CUT 2

CUT 2

FRONT
PANEL

SIDE FRONT
PANEL

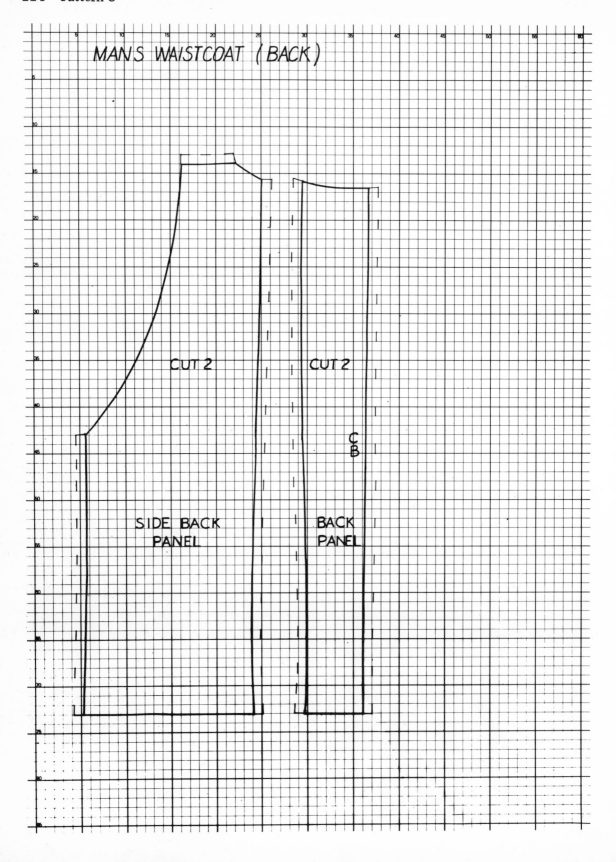

MAN'S WAISTCOAT (BACK)

CUT 2

CUT 2

C
B

SIDE BACK
PANEL

BACK
PANEL

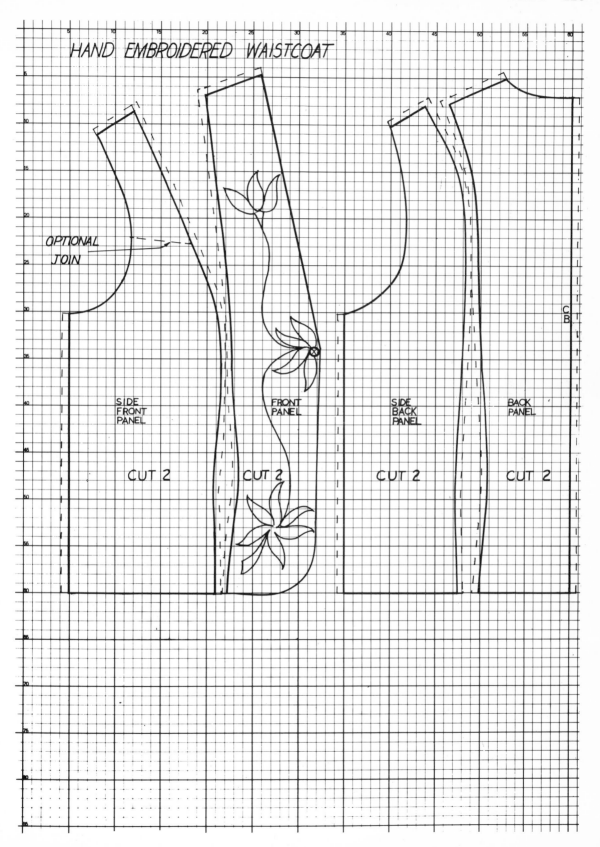

HAND EMBROIDERED WAISTCOAT

OPTIONAL
JOIN

SIDE
FRONT
PANEL

CUT 2

FRONT
PANEL

CUT 2

SIDE
BACK
PANEL

CUT 2

BACK
PANEL

CUT 2

C
B

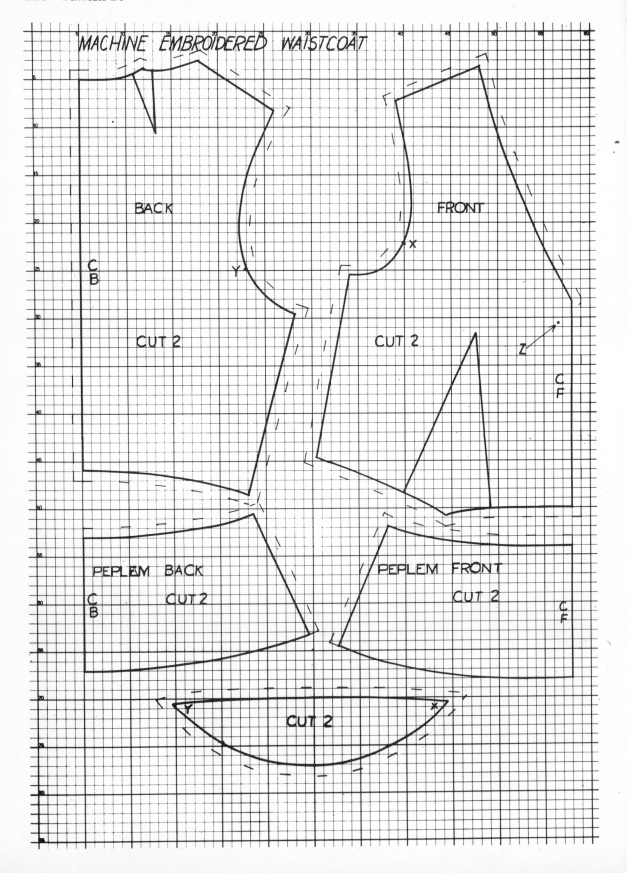

MACHINE EMBROIDERED WAISTCOAT

BACK

FRONT

C
B

CUT 2

CUT 2

C
F

PEPLEM BACK

CUT 2

PEPLEM FRONT

CUT 2

C
B

C
F

CUT 2

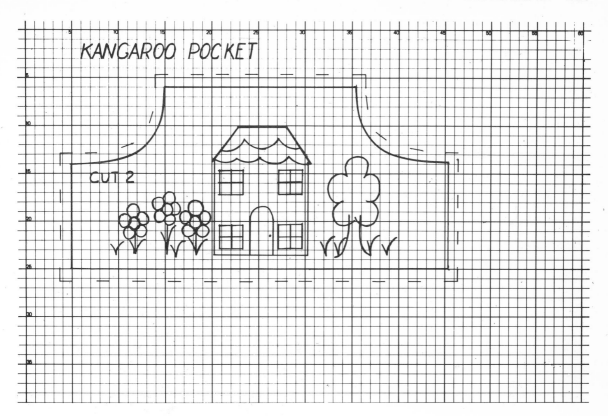

KANGAROO POCKET

CUT 2

Pattern 12

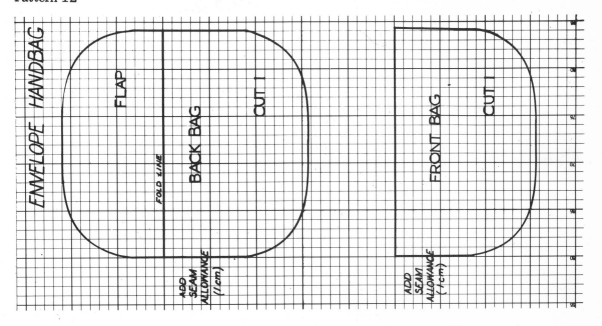

ENVELOPE HANDBAG

FLAP

FOLD LINE

BACK BAG

CUT 1

ADD SEAM ALLOWANCE (1 cm)

FRONT BAG

CUT 1

ADD SEAM ALLOWANCE (1 cm)

# Suppliers

## AUSTRALIAN SUPPLIERS

### Clothing leathers

Leather House Grossman Pty Ltd
80 Campbell Street,
Sydney, NSW

Finest hair sheep, English domestic sheep, Spanish/silk suedes, glove leather and chamois, local garment hides.

Porter & Co Pty Ltd
Leather & Handcraft Supplies
203 Castlereagh Street
Sydney, NSW

Modelling hides, calf skins, kid skins, corrected hides, pig skins, various suedes, chamois. Also large supplier of handcraft tools and accessories.

Platypus Manufacturers Pty Ltd
Cnr Tenterden Road & Margate Street, Botany, NSW

Garment nappa leather

Reynolds Tanning Co Pty Ltd
13 Wilson Street,
Botany, NSW
or Wallace Way,
Chatswood, NSW

Garment suede split from cattle hide, grain leathers from Australian cattle hide, sueded calf skin, chamois, wool on sheepskin suitable for garments. Leather handcraft shops which have accessories for leathercraft.

Mace-Lace Pty Ltd
Leather & Handcraft Supplies
8 Mollison Street,
West End, Qld

Modelling hides, calf skins, kid skins, pig skins, corrected hides, various suedes, chamois. Suppliers of handcraft tools and accessories.

Basnett Garland Pty Ltd
Leather & Grindery Merchants
47 King Street,
Perth, WA

Hides, calf skins kid skins, various suedes, chamois. Suppliers of handcraft tools and accessories.

Bulley & Co
Leather Merchants
380 Elizabeth Street,
Melbourne, Vic

Modelling hides, calf skins, kid skins, corrected hides, various suedes, chamois. Suppliers of handcraft tools and accessories.

Wingfield Hide Curing Co
Plymouth Road,
Wingfield, SA

Leathers, tools and accessories

### Accessories

Most threads and needles for leather sewing can be bought from local haberdashery or handcraft shops. A size 18 sewing machine needle is generally used in Australia.

Some adhesives and glues recommended for use here are: *Selleys Aquadhere, Duall 88* and *Stanford 450 Stainless*. The latter is highly recommended by dry cleaners and is made by Metropolitan Chemical Co, 17 Ralph Street, Alexandria, NSW and other outlets: S.A. Brown Pty Ltd, 50 York Street, Sydney; Muir Gibb Pty Ltd, 393 George Street, Sydney; Mimi Millinery, Cnr Queen and Albert Streets, Brisbane, Qld; L.P. Keating Pty Ltd, 258 Flinders Lane, Melbourne, Vic; A.N. Gilbert Pty Ltd, 713 Hay Street, Perth, WA.

### Dry cleaners

Bliss Dry-Cleaning & Leather Specialist
4 Roslyn Street,
Kings Cross, NSW

Suedecare (Aust) Pty Ltd
771 Elizabeth Street,
Zetland, NSW

V.I.P. Suede & Leather
151 Canterbury Road,
Banktown, NSW

W & M Dry Cleaners
Suede, Leather & Fur Clean Specialists
572 Brunswick Street,
New Farm, Brisbane, Qld

City Dry Cleaners
397 Scarborough Beach Road,
Osborne Park, Perth, WA

Broadway Dry Cleaners
33 Plaza Arcade,
Perth, WA

Shield Dry Cleaners Pty Ltd
36 Brewer Road, Bentleigh, Vic
284 Auburn Road, Auburn, Vic
557 North Road, Ormond, Vic

## NEW ZEALAND SUPPLIERS

Bostik New Zealand Ltd
PO Box 35-093, Naenae
9 Eastern Hutt Road, Lower Hutt

Manufacturers of dies and finishes.

Classic Decor Ltd
PO Box 126, Thames Street,
Napier

Sheepskin products

Glendermid Division of Michaelis
Bayley (NZ) Ltd
PO Box 944,
192-196 Castle Street, Dunedin

This company has warehouses in
Christchurch, Dunedin and
Invercargill. Enquiries would be
welcomed through the Auckland
branch, although they do not
operate a warehouse there.
Stockists of leather for all types
of home handicraft, including
suede clothing leathers and bark
tan, side leather suitable for
shoulder bags, etc.

Outdoor Centre Ltd
PO Box 38017,
282 Jackson Street, Petone

Suppliers of tooling leather, bag
suede. Tandy Leather Craft
embossing and carving tools and
sets. Dyes (spirit and water base),
leather lacquers, finishers and
dressings. Rivets, belt and harness
buckles.

Pacific Leathers (NZ) Ltd
Commission Tanners·
PO Box 870,
Mersey Street, Pandora, Napier

This firm offers garment suedes
and nappas (grain).

Waitaki Leather
PO Box 78,
Oamaru

This firm operates a shop called
'The Craftsman' and has a mail
order service for leather (especially
suede garment leather) and wool-
skins.

## UK SUPPLIERS

J T Batchelor and Co.
39 Nethersall Gardens
Hampstead
London, NW3 5RL

Quality leather, tools and fittings.

S Glassner
(Dept. EAO)
68 Worple Road
Wimbledon
London SW19

Wide range of tools and fittings.
Leather only suitable for accessories.

C and D Hudson
3 Roland Way
Higham Ferrers
Wellingborough
Northamptonshire.

Wide selection of leather pieces
sold by weight. Mail order only.

B H Macready and Co.
14 High Street
Brill
Bucks HP18 9ST

Fashion skins of high quality

John P Milner Ltd
67 Queen Street
Hitchin
Herts

Extensive range of skins,
tools and patterns.

G Tanners Ltd
Bridgehaugh Mill
Selkirk
Scotland TD7 5DR

High quality pigskin clothing
leathers.

U-duit
Church Street
Ripley
Derbyshire

Dyes, tools, punches, books,
leaflets, belt shapes.

# Index